Gerard Manley Hopkins

Gerard Manley Hopkins

a tribute

by W.A.M. Peters, S.J., D.Lit.

Loyola University Press

LIBRARY OF CONGRESS CATALOGING IN PUBLICATION DATA

Peters, William A. M.
    Gerard Manley Hopkins, a tribute.

    1. Hopkins, Gerard Manley, 1844-1889—Criticism and interpretation.
I. Title.
PR4803.H44Z736 1984   821'.8   84-12207
ISBN 0-8294-0456-2

Book design by Carol Tornatore

LOYOLA UNIVERSITY PRESS
3441 North Ashland Avenue
Chicago, IL 60657

amicus Amico

contents

foreword

In 1989 the centenary of the death of Gerard Manley
Hopkins will occur. It is to be expected that a fair number
of essays, perhaps even some books, will commemorate
the life and writings of this poet, who has considerably
grown in stature over the last six decades. This modest
tribute might give the impression of having been written
with the desire to be the first, to beat what is to come. This
is not the case. The reason for its early publication is that
the writer is in frail health, and it is not likely that he will
be privileged to participate in any anniversary celebra-
tion. In honesty he hopes that his admiration for and love
of both poet and poems might inspire others to com-

memorate Hopkins in a way worthy of this loveable person.

I first became acquainted with the poetry of Gerard Manley Hopkins in the early 1930s. At the time I was almost a neighbor of Auden, Spender, and Day-Lewis, who as Oxford undergraduates found themselves rich in the discovery of the startlingly modern poetry of a man who had been dead for almost half a century and whose fifty-odd poems, mostly sonnets, had been published only some fifteen years earlier. Throughout the half century that was to follow, the poet became more and more my wonderful companion. There was an ongoing growth in knowing him better, appreciating him more, even loving him, right across the barrier of death. It happened in a way, I surmise, that is common to many of us.

In the case of a difficult poet, as Hopkins undoubtedly is, I had to make many an effort to grasp what he was trying to convey, to understand his language. But in this way I gained some insight into the experience that prompted and inspired him to express it in verse, and express it in this fashion. This in turn moved me to dig deeper, to penetrate the experience, to discover its roots, to watch its gradual ripening. I was fortunate enough that this made me understand and appreciate the poems better. But in the end there was still something lacking. I had to be very still, learn to listen with the ear, as Hopkins quite often begged his friends to do, and then listen with my whole being, until over many years the communication between poet and reader evolved into tasting, savoring, sharing, and making my own the true and deep experience of the poet. I then discovered that an affinity develops, a certain kinship, in the end, without being either sentimental or arrogant, a friendship.

I confess to a certain hesitancy in using these expressions, the reason being that we were so different. Hopkins was English to the core; I am Dutch. Hopkins was a Victorian; I have lived through the turmoil of the twentieth century. Hopkins was brought up in a deeply religious Anglican family; I was born a Catholic. Hopkins was a man of many talents, including music and drawing; I am no match. To a certain extent these and similar differences were slightly evened out by my wide reading in English literature, by my interest in the history of the Established Church and especially the Oxford Movement, by frequent and lengthy stays in England. I believe that the gap was also narrowed by both of us being priests and by both of us being Jesuits, formed in pretty much the same way, about which more in a later chapter. Hence, with hesitation, and certainly with a great deal of humility, I dedicate this essay: *amicus Amico*: from a friend to a Friend.

The foundation of friendship is never primarily what the friend achieved, not even what he did for his friend; it is not even what the friend gave his friend, what he meant for his friend. Friendship strikes its roots in what the friend *was* and still *is*; this is more than his attractive personality, his admirable character, his talents, perfections, and virtues; any friend's being is always more than the sum of all his achievements and precious qualities.

When any person feels irresistibly drawn to speak or write about his friend, it is unlikely that he gradually moves through his life; he does not care too much about chronology, about succession of events and incidents. It will be more as if he were roaming across a plain, unavoidably, but also of set purpose, visiting and revisiting some favorite spots. To a listener or reader this may strike as repetitiousness, or, worse, evoke the spectre of sentimentality, of over-emotionalism. If this should be the reaction, he does not truly understand friendship. Now, the plain of which I am speaking is never a flawless rose garden. There are dry patches, there are prickly thorn bushes, there may even be an occasional swamp infested with insects, and undoubtedly there will be weeds. A friend is too honest to canonize his friend. He is aware that, however precious and firm the friendship, both parties carry this treasure in earthenware jars. Without this awareness, friendship will sooner or later turn into blind mutual admiration and be no more, or will break into many pieces and be no more.

Once again, turning to the image of the plain, I have indicated my favorite spots by means of the titles given to the chapters of this tribute, *amicus Amico*.

In this essay there will be no footnotes. In my opinion even references to the many quotations taken from Hopkins's poetry are somewhat disturbing. On the other hand, it is irritating to anyone not sufficiently familiar with this poetry to discover that he has to be satisfied with many pairs of inverted commas. So, where Hopkins speaks, I place the number of the poem in parentheses, following the numbering not of the first edition given us by Robert Bridges in 1918, but of the more readily available fourth edition as edited and enlarged by W. H. Gardner and N. H. MacKenzie (Oxford University Press, 1967; paperback edition 1970). Where a quotation is taken from Hopkins's longer poems, *The Wreck of the Deutschland* and *The Loss of the Eurydice*, the reference will be respectively "D" and "L," followed by the number of the stanza.

I make the somewhat bold assumption that the reader is at least to a certain extent acquainted with my thesis: *Gerard Manley Hopkins: A Critical Essay towards the Understanding of his Poetry*, which I finished in 1939 but which because of the Second World War and its subsequent shortage of paper was not published until 1948 (Oxford University Press; second edition 1970). This study concentrated on the implication of Hopkins's own perception of poetry: what I aim at is *inscape*. When in the pages of this tribute I refer the reader to an "elsewhere," it is this study of Hopkins's inscape and instress that I have in mind. Throughout, this tribute finds its nourishment in what I wrote some forty years ago.

Note: I shall be forgiven if in quoting lines from Hopkins's poems I now and again italicize a word, or a few words, where Hopkins used no italics; I could think of no other means to urge the reader to be fully aware of *why this* word is used by the poet in a particular line of verse.

one

the lay-out

On the twenty-first of October 1866, Gerard Manley Hopkins, then in his final year at Balliol College, went from Oxford to Edgbaston along the road that led through historic Woodstock, past Blenheim Palace, through the insignificant villages of Enstone and Chipping Norton, and through Stratford on Avon, where Shakespeare was born. He met with Father John Henry Newman, then a priest belonging to the Society of St. Philip Neri (The Oratorians) and teaching at a boys school very near Birmingham. The purpose of this visit was to be received into the Catholic Church. Hopkins then returned to Oxford, where he finished his studies in the Classics with honors. He was now a "convert," but this at far greater cost than is generally realized. Indeed, we know that it hurt his parents deeply. A little less than twenty years later he still complained bitterly

> Father and mother dear,
> Brothers and sisters are in Christ not near (66).

A conversion is, at times, depicted as a home-coming. This may be true theologically; emotionally it is more often a going into exile. Hopkins lost good friends in Oxford. More important, his conversion cut him off from a Christian communion in which he had been brought up, which he respected. He did not shed what he had loved since he was a child by saying another creed, by substituting the missal for the Book of Common Prayer. He knew that to some his conversion smacked of betraying not merely the Anglican Church, but his country, his own "rare-dear Britain" (D. 35),

> England, whose honour O all my heart woos, wife
> To my creating thought . . . (66).

St. Aloysius's, the church served by the Jesuits, was no St. Mary's, where twenty years earlier Newman preached. And the Douai version of the Bible could in no way compete with the brilliant language of the King James version. True enough, others had taken the step Hopkins took, but still others could not and did not, and men of stature like Pusey and Jowett were still at Oxford. I do not think that Hopkins cherished more admiration for Manning, a converted Archdeacon and now the Archbishop of Westminster, or for the somewhat notorious lay theologian Ward, than for his old friends and masters within the Anglican Communion.

2

From Oxford Hopkins went in 1867 to Edgbaston, under the smoke of Birmingham, not exactly a "towery city and branchy between towers; cuckoo-echoing, bell-swarmèd, lark-charmèd, rook-racked, river- rounded" as Oxford was (44). He became a schoolmaster at the Oratory school, but not for long, mainly, as I have come to know Hopkins, because he just did not have the make-up for teaching and for handling teen-age boys, who then and now are not particularly in love with schoolbenches, nor, for that matter, with Greek and Latin syntax and grammar. In this period he sought Newman's advice about his future: did he have a vocation to be a priest? This possibility was not the result or the concomitant of his conversion. If there had been no conversion, I believe that Hopkins would have joined an Anglican religious community. The evidence appears to be given in two poems which escaped the holocaust when in 1868 he burned the poetry he had written. There is the jewel *Heaven-Haven* (9) with the subtitle: A nun takes the veil. Throughout the eight simple lines of the poem it is easy to discern the poet's own hankering. A couple of years later, in 1866, he wrote *The Habit of Perfection* (22), clearly inspired and pervaded by a gentle yearning for what one now would call religious life.

> ELECTED Silence, sing to me
> And beat upon my whorlèd ear,
> Pipe me to pastures still and be
> The music that I care to hear.
>
> . . . .
>
> And, Poverty, be thou the bride
> And now the marriage feast begun
> And lily-coloured clothes provide
> Your spouse not laboured-at nor spun.

These are the first and the last stanzas of the poem. It should not surprise anyone that Hopkins felt drawn to monastic life, specifically that of the Benedictines; but Newman advised otherwise and was convinced that the Society of Jesus, the order of the Jesuits, was where God wanted him to be.

Following Newman's advice Hopkins applied for admission. This involved an interview with the Superior of the English Province of the Society of Jesus and with three other Jesuits appointed by the Superior. Their task and responsibility was to find out whether this Oxford convert, now twenty-three years of age, had a true vocation to religious life, and if so, to religious life in the Society of Jesus. It is not fanciful to assume that the authority of Newman was of considerable weight in arriving at a decision. Hopkins was accepted; he burned the poetry he had written and decided not to write any more poetry "as alien to his vocation"; in September 1868 he went to Roehampton in southwest London.

At that time Roehampton was a rural village, some six miles from Westminster, hugged-in as it were by Putney Common to the east, Wimbledon Common to the south, and the beauty of Richmond Park to the west. In fact, the spacious grounds of Manresa House, where Hopkins was to stay for two years, are almost part of Richmond Park. Putney was some two miles away, Wimbledon three miles, and Hammersmith with the river Thames also about three miles away. Sixty or seventy years after Hopkins lived there, in the 1930s, not much had changed, except for the traffic and the red double-decker London buses. Now, more than a century later, Roehampton is a London suburb with high-rise buildings, Manresa House has gone, and so have the Jesuits.

The house itself, better the mansion, was named after a little village near Barcelona where the founder of the Society of Jesus, Ignatius of Loyola, on his way to the Holy Land, spent ten months in a grotto praying. It was the year 1522, and his conversion from a rather worldly life as a knight to the life of what he always described as that of a *pobre peregrino* had taken place hardly a year earlier. The mansion was built in neo-classic style, the back facing Richmond Park. However, two out-of-style wings had been added to the right and to the left of the front, thus creating a square in front of the building. They housed the young Jesuits during their first years of formation and the older Jesuits who were in charge of this formation. It is not difficult for me to form a clear idea of the two years that Hopkins spent at Manresa House, the reason being that when I came to live there for a year in the very early 1930s, little had changed. The great turn-around, both as regards the formation itself and the locality, came after the Second World War. It was in Manresa House that I heard the name Gerard Manley Hopkins for the first time. This did not happen when the young Jesuit students conversed with each other during the time set aside for recreation. Rather, at the time a certain Father Donohue came to live at Manresa House. He was the gentlest of Jesuits of an older generation, well into his seventies, which means that he was some fifteen years younger than Hopkins. But he had known Gerard Manley, not as a poet but as an amiable fellow Jesuit. To my perennial regret I did not sit down for hours at the feet of this humble Jesuit, because Hopkins was no more to me then than a name which was hardly ever heard. Some few years later at Manresa House I met W. H. Gardner, the author of the *magnum opus* in two volumes, published by the Oxford University Press during the war, and editor of *Poems of Gerard Manley Hopkins* (third enlarged edition, 1948). At the time he was a schoolmaster in East Sheen, a London suburb, and he came to visit Father Donohue regularly. It was Father Donohue who received Mr. Gardner into the Catholic Church.

I had my first inspiring conversation about Hopkins with Mr. Gardner. He was working on his two volumes and I was rather anxious to know what he had in mind. He gave me the impression that he intended to cover pretty well all the aspects of both the life and the poetry of Hopkins. I was intensely interested in what he was going to write because by that time some primitive outlines of my own study of Hopkins's poetry were taking shape. I was aware of the possibility that two writers could be covering the same material. My anxiety proved to be groundless.

Alfred Thomas, a Jesuit himself, has written a scholarly work: *Hopkins the Jesuit* (Oxford University Press, 1969). It is a standard work, and the few remarks that I feel drawn to make are of a more personal nature. Hopkins's transition from Oxford to Roehampton was not easy. He was twenty-four and found himself in a community of fellow novices, most of whom were little more than grown-up boys of about eighteen. Now, in a novitiate no exceptions are made because of age, or Oxford degree, or for that matter because of conversion. It cannot have been easy for Hopkins to adapt himself to the devotional practices and pious ways of acting which were meant to shape the novices who were not only much younger than he but unavoidably less mature, and far less acquainted with suffering. Evidently, he was well liked; otherwise he would not have been a kind of liaison officer between the novices and their novice master.

Life at Roehampton will seem rather forbidding to an outsider, almost inhuman: rise at 5:40 (no one had a private room; it was dormitory living); after a visit to the chapel, an hour's mental prayer; this was followed by Mass. At eight o'clock the novices walked in silence through what was called The Gallery to the dining hall, high-ceilinged, plain long tables lining the walls, and a pulpit half-way up the wall in the middle of the refectory whence the reading took place. The meal was taken in silence. It was sober (no trace of bacon and eggs, except for some of the priests), and the novices did the serving. In the course of the morning the novices spent half an hour in spiritual reading, the classic book being *Christian Perfection* by Father Alphonsus Rodriguez, the Jesuit who wrote it more than two and a half centuries earlier. They then listened to an explanation of the Constitutions of the Society of Jesus and the rules. They did manual work that ranged from washing dishes and helping in the kitchen to sweeping leaves in the fall: in general, keeping the house clean. With half an hour's precious *free time* thrown in, the morning ended at twelve-thirty. Half an hour was then spent in prayer (examination of conscience!), and dinner was at one. The angelus-bell took the novices to the refectory, where the midday meal was taken, again in silence, with one of the young members reading from a spiritual book. The books selected were traditionally of high quality, and in the course of any Jesuit's formation—and thereafter—he listened to excellent books which otherwise he might possibly never have heard of.

After dinner the novices were given their first opportunity to converse with one another, outdoors, weather permitting, in groups of three. In the course of the afternoon there was another period of manual work, a little study or another conference, a break for tea with dry bread, and in the evening another hour devoted to prayer. Supper was at eight, followed by recreation. The day ended with no less than three-quarters of an hour for prayer, which was divided up in saying together with the priests and the brothers the Litany of the Saints, in privately preparing one's mental prayer of next morning, and finally an examination of conscience. A healthy amount of physical exercise was woven into the weekly schedule. There was little contact with one's relatives and friends; writing was rationed; visits were rare.

It may not have been an easy life, but it was not a hard life. There were outstanding compensations, not just those of a spiritual nature, not merely those of peace and quiet and a rather carefree existence, but, above all, although at times overlooked, of precious friendships. Years and years afterwards Jesuits still feel close to their fellow novices, and this is easy to explain. From a merely human point of view novices had nothing—nothing except each other, and this made for friendship, often enduring friendship. They lived together, they worked together, they prayed together, they shared hardships; they listened together when every month a summary of the Constitutions of Ignatius and the rules were read in the dining hall.

Hopkins's life as a young Jesuit took its normal course. He finished the first period of his formation, the novitiate, after two years and took his vows of perpetual poverty, chastity, and obedience in September 1870. Being somewhat older and having his Oxford degree, he was exempted from the two years of humanistic studies in Manresa House, known as the juniorate, and he went to Stonyhurst to study philosophy for the next three years. Roehampton was London; Stonyhurst at that time was nowhere. It was some twelve miles east of Preston, some ten miles north of Blackburn, in Ribblesdale country, which he was to describe as

> EARTH, sweet Earth, sweet landscape, with leavès throng
> And louchèd low grass ... (58).

Not far away the Hodder River made the countryside a land of "wet and of wildness" which he loved so much and of which he sang some twenty years later when he visited Inversnaid in Scotland:

> What would the world be, once bereft
> Of wet and of wildness? Let them be left,
> O let them be left, wildness and wet;
> Long live the weeds and the wilderness yet (56).

I would give a false impression if Stonyhurst were to stand for wilderness. It was for all practical purposes Stonyhurst College, a Catholic public school for boys of well-to-do parents, run by Jesuits. The school had a history that went back to the time of the persecution of the Catholics, when boys were sent to St. Omer's in France. Half a century before Hopkins moved up to North Lancashire, the boys had stormed the grim grey stone building—castle is perhaps the better word—and occupied it, up till today. At this time Hopkins had nothing whatsoever to do with the school (he would in later years). There was another building, to the side of the college, undistinctive and, given the climate, rather bleak for many months each year. It was St. Mary's Hall. It was here that Hopkins spent the next three years, given to the study of philosophy.

9

There was more privacy, more freedom here than at Manresa House; more time was now devoted to the intellectual formation of the young Jesuit. But, on the whole, life did not differ much from that of Manresa House. Manual work and spiritual conferences were replaced by lectures in philosophy, and the time for prayer was slightly shortened. But the daily routine of rising, mental prayer, Mass, breakfast and other meals, and periods of recreation was pretty much as Hopkins had known it in Roehampton. As regards his lectures and his study, the first year was mainly given to logic and ontology, the second to psychology and cosmology, the final year to ethics and natural theology. The master was Thomas Aquinas (c. 1227-74), who built his philosophical system more on Aristotle than on Plato. Outwardly Hopkins moved smoothly along with his fellow students, and few, if any, were aware what profound change was actually taking place in him, and this in the deepest recesses of his being. He came across the Franciscan philosopher, Duns Scotus (c. 1265-1308), whom he was to call "of realty the rarest-veinèd unraveller" (44). This could only mean that to Hopkins Scotus was somehow as fascinated by the individual as he was himself. "At this time I had first begun to get hold of the copy of Scotus on the Sentences . . . and was flush with a new stroke of enthusiasm. It may come to nothing or it may be a mercy of God. But just then when I took in any inscape of the sky or sea I thought of Scotus," he wrote in his diary under August the third, 1872. It is an interesting date because Hopkins had now finished his second year in St. Mary's Hall, and it was holiday time. Not many of his fellow Jesuits would take up any book on philosophy at that time of the year.

I do not think that this encounter with Duns Scotus

was like an explosion, breaking open a new world. It came more like a gentle confirmation on the level of the intellect of what had lived in his heart and mind for many, many years. Neither do I think that Hopkins's sharing Scotus's thought and vision was simply a source of joy and peace. No longer knowing himself to be a true and faithful follower of Thomas Aquinas, he set himself aside from his brother Jesuits, and he was wise enough not to noise it abroad that he could not agree and move along with his professors. It was wise for him not to say anything about this and to keep to himself what to him was a treasure, to others a deviation. This makes for a certain loneliness, so that even in this unexpected area there must already have been a trace of "to seem the stranger lies my lot" (66). We know that he suffered because others did not share his vision of reality: people went on hacking and hewing down aspens dear (43), and went on to thriftless reave the rich round world bare and thus make earth wear brows of care and dear concern (58), went on searing, blearing, smearing God's Grandeur with trade and toil, making nature wear man's smudge and share man's smell (31). All this grieved him, but it never quite depressed him, because he knew "there lives the dearest freshness deep down things" (31).

What has always surprised me is that this confirmation of the preciousness of the individual, of inscape and instress, did not come earlier. It is indeed unlikely that Hopkins read Newman's *A Grammar of Assent* when it appeared in 1870, the reason being that this kind of book was not given a place in the library of the novitiate. But once at Stonyhurst Hopkins must surely have known of Newman's latest work with its cardinal distinction between notional and real assent, between the notional and

11

the real, with its underlying emphasis that man does not believe with his intellect alone but with his whole being. There is a clear affinity between the way in which Newman approached and viewed reality and the way in which Hopkins did. Apparently they were here like ships that pass in the night. I shall return to the relationship between these two great men in a later chapter.

When a young Jesuit has finished his course of philosophy, and before he is sent to start four years of theological studies, it is common procedure for him to be moved either to a university to work for his M.A. or Ph.D., or to a Jesuit high school to teach for two or three years. Now and again an English scholastic—the name given to this young Jesuit—finds himself back in Roehampton to teach the Juniors, those who have just finished their two-year novitiate. This happened to Hopkins, but the great difference this made in his life is that he now belonged to the community of his fellow professors, all of them priests, all of them older, some of them considerably older. It was not an unexpected assignment, when we consider Hopkins's degree, his age, and his brilliant mind, which by now was evident both to his superiors and to his contemporaries.

Hopkins taught at Roehampton for only one year, in all likelihood because by now he was getting on toward thirty. When in the fall of 1874 he went to St. Beuno's College in North Wales to begin his theological studies, he had passed the thirty mark. St. Beuno's was a rather inaccessible place, but that was for most students the least of tribulations. It was not an attractive house; it had a certain gloominess about it, and from this point of view it fitted in well with the surroundings, especially when for many months the weather was bleak and cold, and not many students were as fond of "wet and wildness" as Hopkins was. The remarkable aspect of the poet's three years at St. Beuno's is that somehow he blossomed: he started singing and began writing poetry. When I try to find the source of an unmistakable exuberance, I do not think that the study of theology accounts for it; its over-emphasis on dogma and moral theology could never be very exciting or inspiring. Neither do I think that the prospect of ordination to the priesthood gives an expla-nation, nor the fact that Hopkins considered himself free to write poetry. It may take a flower a long time to develop; then suddenly in the course of a day or a night, it springs into full bloom. I like to think that is what happened to Hopkins.

At the same time, no one should romanticize Hop-kins's stay at St. Beuno's. What I called exuberance was not pure, unpolluted joy; it was shot through with pain. To a careful reader there are few poems written in Wales that are not tinged with sorrow. *Pied Beauty*, yes, but it is an exception. *Hurrahing in Harvest* makes us expect an outburst of triumph over everything that is unpleasant, painful, and ugly. Yet, even here, having mentioned the rich glory of harvest time, Hopkins adds, in my reading somewhat sadly,

> These things, these things were here and but the beholder
> Wanting . . . (38).

where I like to draw the attention to the repetition of *these things*, stressing their beauty, and to the word *wanting*; it does not merely stand for *being absent*, but also for *being the poorer for it*, or for *missing so much*.

For another reason, there was not too much at St. Beuno's to **grow** romantic about. Here was **gathered** together a group of men, roughly between the ages thirty and thirty-five, still in school benches, and after twelve to fifteen years still in formation. (Hopkins himself had not been that long in the Society of Jesus, only six years when he began his course in theology.) The daily schedule, again, did not differ significantly from that of the previous years. It was still rising at the early hour, all at the same time; then, as before, an hour's mental prayer, followed by Mass and breakfast in silence. The morning hours were given to attending classes and private study; prayer before the midday meal, taken in silence, followed by recreation. The afternoon and evening were again given to lectures and study with more time for a tea break. And at the end of the long day again three-quarters of an hour devoted to prayer.

After the discovery of Scotus, Hopkins could not be fascinated by the rational approach to the various theological treatises going by, even for non-Latinists, understandable titles: *De Deo Uno et Trino*, *De Deo Creatore*, *De Deo Redemptore*, *De Sacramentis*, and so on. Theology was to an unhealthy extent proof, then refutation of the adversaries (the schismatics and heretics!). This was often by means of Scriptural texts which were completely taken out of context, bolstered up by passages taken from the Fathers of the Church (also often taken out of context) and theologians of an earlier age. Scripture was almost exclusively exegesis, and moral theology reduced the problems and the pains of men and women (going by the names *Titus* and *Barbara*) to "cases," and the *case* had to be solved when it was assumed that now the *persons* were helped. Moral theology was oriented toward preparing the young priests for the confessional. As regards Church history, the great historical works had yet to be

written (Pastor). It is little wonder, then, that in the correspondence of these years Hopkins wrote about literature,
that in his diary of these years he showed how he had
fallen in love with all things beautiful (37). As Scotus
broke a certain monotony in his Stonyhurst years, so a
chance remark made by his rector expressing the wish
that someone would write about the tragedy of the
Deutschland (wrecked near the estuary of the Thames on
the seventh of December in 1875) brought life to his years
at St. Beuno's. He now considered himself free to write
poetry.

It would not be surprising, given the long formation
and the age of the students as well as the unattractiveness
to many of the curriculum, that boredom would set in. I
do not think that this was the case, and not just with
Hopkins. There was too much friendship for this to
happen; there were too many mature men among one's
companions. Some were to become famous after a de-
cade or so: the brothers Rickaby, Keating, Thurston (still
famous, or rather notorious, in the 1930s), Considine,
Galway, Bacon, and many others. Above all, there was a
growing impatience: the priesthood was now not too far
away. In a manner of speaking, the end of the road came
into sight, and this makes for an encouraging and
exhilarating experience.

Gerard Manley Hopkins was ordained a priest on
the twenty-third of September 1877; he was thirty-three
years old. But ordination is not the end of a Jesuit's
formation. There follows a fourth year of theological
studies, and normally this is followed by the so-called
tertianship, about which more in a moment. At this point
Hopkins's formation and life take a different route.

Immediately after his ordination Hopkins was to

work for the next four years in Jesuit parishes in London, Glasgow, Bedford Leigh, Liverpool, and Oxford. It is well known that those years were no easy time, and the many moves from one place to another might suggest that he was nowhere a success. This is, however, not necessarily so. The many moves may also indicate that he was not given a permanent assignment anywhere because he had not yet made his tertianship and no one could tell when he might be called back to Roehampton for this second probation or second novitiate. Parish work was undoubtedly hard. It was not just that Hopkins was far too sensitive to feel at ease and comfortable where

> ...all is seared with trade; bleared, smeared with toil;
> And wears man's smudge and shares man's smell (31)

and where there was much poverty, and worse, drunkenness, and other repulsive vices. At the time he wrote to his friend Dixon: "My Liverpool and Glasgow experience laid upon my mind a conviction, a truly crushing conviction, of the misery of town life to the poor and more than to the poor, of the misery of the poor in general, of the degradation even of our race, of the hollowness of this century's civilization." It was all a far cry from the milieu in which he had been brought up. He wrote little poetry in these years (1878-81), except in 1879 when he was in Oxford and gave us nine poems, the first one being a lament for his *Binsey Poplars* (43) and the last one another lament about his lack of peace (51). Another few were written when he was on holiday (54, 55, 56).

To understand Hopkins's life during these four years, one must appreciate, apart from the uncertainty of where he would be next year, the drastic change in his everyday existence. For the first time since his high-school days he was away from books and from school benches (except for his one year as professor of the juniors). For the first time since he entered the Society of Jesus, now nine years ago, he lived as a priest in a small community of Jesuit priests. For the first time since he went to Roehampton, he did not live a well-ordered daily schedule; apart from fixed times for meals, the pastor had to schedule his own day, very much depending upon the demands made by his parishoners. For the first time in his life—and he was now thirty-three—he bore responsibility for people who trusted him, who relied upon his help, encouragement, wisdom, and guidance as they came to him with their sins, their failures, their sufferings, and their problems. No one can afford to lose sight of the fact that he spent many an hour in the confessional. In his letters we now hear him refer to fatigue, weariness, and ill health too. Yet we catch a glimpse of the good priest he was in a poem written in Liverpool. A parishioner, a blacksmith by trade, had died:

This seeing the sick endears them to us, us too it endears.
My tongue had taught thee comfort, touch had quenched
     thy tears,
Thy tears that touched my heart, child, Felix, poor Felix
     Randal (53).

Finally—because as we pointed out, it is not common in the Society of Jesus to delay the tertianship for four years—Hopkins went back to Roehampton, where he had entered thirteen years earlier. The tertianship lasts ten months, and for Ignatius its main purpose was for the Jesuit to regain his first fervor if long years of study might have cooled this. Ignatius called this year *schola affectus*. Opinions differ as to what he meant exactly by that expression, and it cannot be simply identified as a *schola orationis*, a school of prayer; in this case Ignatius would have used this simpler expression. Indeed, prayer, solitude, and spiritual reading were given a very prominent place. As I understand Ignatius, the *schola affectus* was a school for learning how to handle being "affected" by God; that is, how to handle the mystery of the *Spiritual Exercises*; that is, the mystery of God communicating directly with the devout person, disposing him, even embracing him, moving, stirring, and enlightening him, consoling him, and this at times "without any preceding cause." These words are all taken from the text of the *Spiritual Exercises*. It is dangerous to use the expression "mystical prayer," but this is undoubtedly what Ignatius had in mind. From Hopkins's notes on the *Spiritual Exercises*, we know that this is the way he understood Ignatius, and he was well ahead of his time in understanding him in this way. I like to add that all prayer takes its initiative with God, not with any man (see Romans 8:26), and that as a result any prayer is in its very root mystical. There will be an increase of degree, of intensity, but there will be no change of essence. Hence, the question of whether Hopkins was a mystic or became one in his Dublin years posits to me a non-existent problem.

Since the year spent by Hopkins in making his tertianship is not easy to understand for the outsider, I fall back upon what Hopkins wrote to Dixon: "It is in preparation for these last vows that we make the tertianship; which is called *schola affectus* and is meant to enable us to recover that fervour which may have cooled through application to study and contact with the world. . . . Besides all which, my mind is here more at peace than it has ever been and I would gladly live all my life, if it were so to be, in as great or greater seclusion from the world and be busied only with God. But in the midst of outward occupations not only the mind is drawn away from God, which may be at the call of duty and be God's will, but unhappily the will too is entangled, worldly interests freshen, and worldly ambitions revive. The man who in the world is as dead to the world as if he were buried in the cloister is already a saint. But this is our ideal." Hopkins was repeatedly reminded of this ideal whenever he listened to the Constitutions and the rules of the Society. Ignatius emphasizes the *maxima familiaritas cum Deo*, and the *instrumentum intime conjunctum cum Deo*, words that need no translation.

At the end of his tertianship Hopkins was assigned to Stonyhurst College. He had been away from the spacious grounds, playing fields, and the somewhat foreboding buildings for eight years. This time he was not to reside in St. Mary's Hall, but in the school itself. His was not a schoolmaster's life as we are inclined to understand this. In those days the older boys were given courses in philosophy—would you believe it?—and this special group went by the name of *secular philosophers*. Hopkins was to teach them for two years, and we can only speculate what this Scotistic philosopher handed on. We do know from his fellow Jesuits that he was well liked, notwithstanding a streak of being different, which was attributed to his predilection for art, be it architecture, drawing, or music. It is interesting that few if any were aware of his poetry. No wonder, because his *Wreck of the Deutschland* was refused by the Jesuit periodical *The Month*, and after that Hopkins never offered anything else for publication. But he did write a few poems. *Ribblesdale* is dated Stonyhurst 1882, and I believe that the opening lines of

As kingfishers catch fire (57) point to his stay at Stonyhurst. We know for certain that he laid his hand at this time to what he hoped would be his *magnum opus, The Drama of St. Winefred*. In the end it proved too much for him, and we have only two fragments, about one of which he wrote: "I never did anything more musical" (59; see also 152). It was customary at Stonyhurst for the boys to place their little poetic efforts before the statue of the Virgin Mary during the month of May. *The May Magnificat* (42) may have been written for this purspose. His lengthy poem *The Blessed Virgin compared to the Air we Breathe* (60) may in a similar way have found its way to the end of the long corridor where the statue of Mary was decorated in May.

By this time Hopkins was involved in a fairly regular correspondence with Robert Bridges, his friend from Oxford days, and with Canon Dixon, to whom he had written to express his appreciation of Dixon's poems. From this correspondence it is clear that Hopkins was an avid reader, this in a scholarly sense of the word. It is also clear that he had more than a passing acquaintance with Keats, Tennyson, Wordsworth, Browning, "that plague" Swinburne, with Dickens ("too mawkish"), Ruskin, Carlyle, and, no surprise, Shakespeare and Milton. These were writers about whom in his correspondence he gave his fair and critical assessment. It is quite safe to assume that Shelley, Byron, and the Pre-Raphaelites were also read, as were, and this we know for certain, Stevenson and Hardy.

In 1884, when he turned forty, Hopkins was made professor of Latin and Greek at University College in Dublin. We know that he did not like his stay in Dublin at all. Hence it is good to be aware of his reaction when asked to go to Dublin.

It was soon after the restoration of the hierarchy, 1850, that the English bishops were faced with the problem of whether it was safe to send Catholic young men to Oxford. Newman was for it, but he lost his cause, and, rather ironically, he was asked to begin a Catholic university in Dublin for both Irish and English Catholic young men. In 1852 he gave his famous lectures on *The Idea of a University*. He gathered together a staff, many of whom were English and converts, and it was trouble from the beginning. Six years later, in 1858, Newman resigned and returned to his Birmingham Oratory. All this took place when Hopkins was a schoolboy; but when he came to Oxford, to be an undergraduate and a Catholic amounted more or less to being disobedient to the Archbishop of Westminster, ex-Archdeacon Manning. Now Hopkins was sent to teach at a university created from nothing by Newman, which disowned him half a dozen years later.

It cannot have been very attractive to Hopkins, who respected Newman. Moreover, it is surely unthinkable that Hopkins could have forgotten the turmoil when Newman answered the attack made by Canon Kingsley: *What, Then, Does Dr. Newman Mean?*; the question clearly implied that Newman was no better than a liar. Newman replied with what is generally considered a masterpiece of autobiography, *Apologia Pro Vita Sua* (April 11 to May 2, 1864, in seven parts). Notice that at this time Hopkins was finishing his first year at Balliol. To me it is unbelievable that the clash between Kingsley and Newman left Hopkins undisturbed. After all, Kingsley was a man of authority; he was canon of Westminster, a well-known writer, although not much to Hopkins's liking. For the canon, although a member of the officially established Anglican Church, was hardly of the same religious persuasion as Newman, when he was still a member of that Church, or as Hopkins, who was brought up in and was still very much attached to what is called the High Church, and who was now undoubtedly influenced by the Oxford Movement. Within three years Hopkins was to ask Newman to receive him into the Catholic Church.

Besides, we know how deeply concerned Hopkins remained about his Alma Mater. Oxford always remained to him Duns Scotus's Oxford. It is only natural to assume that Hopkins must have been elated when a few months after his ordination Trinity College, Oxford, made Newman an Honorary Fellow. Hopkins was actually in Oxford when Newman was created a cardinal in May of 1879. And now in 1884 Hopkins is sent to what was Newman's great and most painful failure (in the eyes of some) or a cruel disappointment (in his own experience) that went by the name of University College, Dublin.

Hopkins was, of course, aware of the turbulent history of this university, aware also that Newman wanted to found an Oratory and a Catholic Centre in Oxford, even bought some property for this purpose, and all this with the support of his Bishop Ullathorne of Birmingham. In the end Rome intervened, presumably at the instigation of Manning and the lay-theologian Ward; that was the end of a project Newman cherished and which he knew would be of great benefit to the Catholic young men, who by that time were allowed to study at Oxford University. We must not lose sight of the fact that all this took place when Hopkins himself was still an Oxford undergraduate. It is unreasonable to assume that these sad events were erased from Hopkins's mind when he went to Dublin. There was still the church on St. Stephen's

Green, built by Newman as a university chapel, to remind him of them.

Unfortunately for Hopkins, Dublin was in Ireland. Not that he had any grudge against the Irish (many of whom he had helped when he worked in Liverpool, Bedford Leigh, and Glasgow), but with his intense love for his "rare-dear Britain" (D. 35), one cannot be surprised that he felt exiled, at least a stranger (66). By the time a Jesuit has been a member of his province within the Society for almost twenty years, he knows, and is known to, the vast majority of his fellow Jesuits in that province; his life is enriched by the friendship of many. If he moves to another province, even one next door, as happened to Hopkins in 1884, he hardly knows a soul. He finds himself in a community of Jesuits who are names and in a province where he is a stranger. It takes time before he feels at ease and at home, and it must have taken a man of Hopkins's shy character quite a while before he reached that point. As a matter of fact, it is a legitimate question whether he ever truly felt comfortable in the University College community. Adjustment makes great demands and is nourished by a good deal of energy. Here Hopkins was at a disadvantage. He was never of robust health; in the first years of his life as a priest he complains, we have seen, of feeling tired, jaded, and weary. Somewhat later he wrote of being in a state of delapidation, of prostration of strength. As if all this were not a heavy enough cross to bear, there was no ambition in Hopkins. Others might see being a university professor as an achievement, something to be proud of; to Hopkins it was only a burden. He was never cut out to be a teacher, at whatever level. One can be too diligent in preparing one's classes and lectures, and the notes we still possess demonstrate that the job was too arduous for Hopkins and that sooner or later he would break down. If any master cannot decide whether the paper of his student should be graded seventy-two or seventy-four and feels compelled to do the marking all over again, and cannot in conscience make the bold decision to split the difference, he had better find another job. It was Hopkins's exaggerated, even scrupulous, sense of honesty that made him lose many a good night's sleep just to find out whether he had been, again, scrupulously fair in marking a paper. Thus no one assumes that Hopkins's journey to Dublin constituted a pleasant change, or stood for a well-deserved promotion from being a master at a secondary school to a real university. In all likelihood the change itself was the herald of worse to come, and such forebodings proved to be all too correct.

This sensitive, somewhat over-conscientious man had never lived in any one community for more than three years. He was three years as a student of philosophy at St. Mary's Hall and three years as a student of theology at St. Beuno's. These two periods fell within the first nine years of his life as a Jesuit. Of the eight years that were to follow his stay in North Wales, he spent two in Stonyhurst College and a little less than two at St. Aloysius's Church in Oxford. For what remained he was practically moved around every year. All this is rather exceptional for a Jesuit. After his formation he is usually assigned to a school, a retreat house, a parish, a professorate, and more often than not he remains at that post until his death. To be a master or a professor in the same house and at the same task for forty years is by no means exceptional. It is what a Jesuit more or less expects. Going from place to place is generally taken to be a sign of not being quite a success, to put it mildly; so he is wisely given another chance somewhere else. Hopkins was to stay five whole years in Dublin, until his death, in the same place, with the same task, neither of which was much to his liking. This was, however, not the only reason that he referred to these years as his "winter world" in the last sonnet he wrote, dedicated to his friend Robert Bridges (76). That it played a painful part cannot be doubted.

In the spring of 1889 Hopkins was struck by typhoid fever; he died peacefully in a foreign country on the eighth of June. He was buried in Glasnevin Cemetery, and laid to rest, as the expression goes, among his fellow Jesuits. A large tombstone mentions their names and most inconspicuously among them I find the name *Gerard Manley Hopkins*, followed by date of birth and date of death. To me it is a place in a cemetery where I love to go and stand and think and recite poems to myself; it is as dear to me as the cemetery where my parents are buried. The plaque in the poets' corner of Westminster Abbey, a 1975 tribute to Hopkins, the poet of *The Wreck of the Deutschland*, from his other lovers and friends and admirers never moves me in this way.

This brings me to the end of what I called the "lay-out." It reminds me somehow of the barn "within doors house the shocks" (32). From it comes to me the invitation "come you indoors, come home," with a slight shift in the meaning these words have in his poem *The Candle Indoors* (46). To a friend the lay-out is little more than the framework; it is not his friend's home. But it is in his home that the treasures are found that create and nourish, in an ever-ongoing way, true friendship. A tribute is mainly concerned with these treasures. I have named some of them, using Hopkins's own words; they are the titles of the chapters to come.

two

"*on Saturday sailed from Bremen. . .*"

It appears that there is no starting point so obvious, perhaps unavoidable, for any tribute as some enlightening, inspiring remarks and observations about *The Wreck of the Deutschland*. It is the poem with which in 1875 Hopkins broke his self-imposed restrictions not to write any more poetry as alien to his vocation, a decision taken in 1868 when after burning the poems he had written he entered the Society of Jesus. To not a few, Hopkins has become identical with this poem of thirty-five irregular and jumpy-looking stanzas. I have joined the throng of Hopkins admirers who, grateful for having given much time and energy to master its language and contents, know themselves richly rewarded. But is, then, the title of this chapter not ill chosen? Would the majestic poetry of

> THOU mastering me
> God! giver of breath and bread;
> World's strand, sway of the sea

not have been more appropriate? Or

> Thou art lightning and love, I found it, a winter and warm
> (9)?

Maybe to some, but not to me. The matter-of-factness of the twelfth stanza stands in sharp contrast with the solemnity of the opening lines of the poem, and with many other impressive, even harrowing lines. But the stark simplicity of the statement "On Saturday sailed from Bremen, American-outward-bound . . . " has made me understand, appreciate, and love Hopkins as a person and a poet more than the eleven preceding stanzas or all the so-called "terrible sonnets." The reason will come to friends and critics as a surprise as it did to me. I have to add that it was not the beginning of this twelfth stanza that gave me, unexpectedly, a deeper understanding of Hopkins. To a large extent the same result was effected by the opening lines of many other poems; much of his early poetry stirred me in a similar way:

> THE world is charged with the grandeur of God.
> It will flame out, like shining from shook foil (31).

> I CAUGHT this morning morning's minion, king-
> dom of daylight's dauphin, dapple-dawn-drawn Falcon,
> . . . (36).

> I REMEMBER a house where all were good
> To me, God knows, deserving no such thing (34).

SUMMER ends now; now, barbarous in beauty, the
stooks rise
Around; up above, what wind-walks . . . (38).

SOMETIMES a lantern moves along the night.
    That interests our eyes. And who goes there?
    I think; where from and bound, I wonder, where,
                                        (40).

SOME candle clear burns somewhere I come by.
I muse at how its being puts blissful back
With yellowy moisture mild night's blear-all black (46).

THE Eurydice—it concerned thee, O Lord:
Three hundred souls, O alas! on board, . . . (41).

FELIX RANDALL the farrier, O is he dead then?
    my duty all ended,
Who have watched his mould of man, big-boned and
    hardy-handsome
Pining, pining, . . . (53).

A BUGLER boy from barrack (it is over the hill
There) . . . (48).

So many more examples might be added. What do these
lines, so divergent, have in common? They made it clear
to me that the greater part of Hopkins's poetry is *narrative* poetry. This would meet with no denial when we have
in mind *The Wreck of the Deutschland*, *The Loss of the
Eurydice*, *The Bugler's First Communion*, the hopelessly un-
finished *St. Winefred's Well*, or even *Brothers* (resp. 48, 59,
54). But many lines quoted just now are taken from short
poems, most of them sonnets, and to associate the writing
of sonnets with narrative poetry, with telling a story,
appears to be stretching the very meaning of narrative.

29

People will qualify the early sonnets as nature poetry; listen to the titles: *The Starlight Night, Spring, The Sea and the Skylark, The Windhover, Pied Beauty, Hurrahing in Harvest* (resp. 32, 33, 35, 36, 37, 38). Yet, when I now read and in the past began to read the lines above, and what followed after such an opening, I could not help being reminded over and over again of a child coming home and eagerly telling mom and dad of what had happened. The child does not give information, nor make statements; no, there is the telling of a story. This is often the difference between children and adults, especially journalists who claim to go in for *stories*, but in actual fact hardly ever move beyond giving information about the accident, or the brush fire, or whatever event. They are too little the child and too much the sophisticated adult to be able to *narrate* what happened, what they experienced.

Now, notice the simple childlike straightforwardness of Hopkins. Moved, impelled by the uncomplicated need to have others share what he saw, what filled him with surprise and joy, what made him cry, he expresses himself with a directness that looks almost like buttonholing the reader, urging him to listen. I am well aware that it is foolish to rank Hopkins with Homer or Virgil, or, closer to home, Chaucer or Milton. From the point of view of volume, he certainly does not belong in their class. Yet, a good listener, reading with the ear, will soon find himself like a child, for only a child knows how to listen to a story well told, and only a child is eager for another story, where adults turn to the newspaper. The conclusion is very important: Hopkins's poetry will not be properly understood and loved until at least the majority of his poems have become means of communication between a child and a child.

30

This sounds rather presumptuous, especially when one main objection is that Hopkins is anything but like a child: just look at the language he used! This has to be admitted—although one must not exaggerate as I shall clarify later—but to a certain extent we now beg the question: the language is unnecessarily difficult to many readers because they fail to approach Hopkins's poems as stories, because they fail to come to Hopkins as a child, the attractive child that he was in the depth of his being. By way of illustration: let the reader once again take *The Windhover* (36) or *The Lantern out of Doors* (40) or *The Handsome Heart* (47); I do not think that the strongly narrative element will strike him. The trouble is, of course, that few readers will take any sonnet in hand and expect that they should be listening as children to a story. Normally, they know that they are invited to be moved by the description of a flower, or by Chapman's Homer or by Bridges's high esteem of Hopkins (the introductory sonnet to his edition of Hopkins's poems). They are supposed to share the emotions of the poet, or are asked to listen to what amounts to an exhortation or a camouflaged sermon, with a couple of punch lines at the very end. But why did Hopkins insist so persistently that his poetry was not to be read but to be heard with the ear? This persistency implies an unmistakable urgent appeal: "Please, listen to me." Surely, if poetry is communication of an experience or clarification of a statement, what has the ear to do with it?

It is not unthinkable that at this point Hopkins readers and Hopkins scholars will point out that the poet does preach rather than narrate, and this in all his early poetry. Examples:

> Be adored among men,
> God, three-numberèd form;

Wring thy rebel, dogged in den,
  Man's malice, with wrecking and storm (D. 9).

Narrative, or part of a sermon?

Let him easter in us, be a dayspring to the dimness of us,
  be a crimson-cresseted east,
More brightening her, rare-dear Britain, . . . (D. 35).

Narrative? Sermon? Prayer?

And though the last lights off the black West went
  Oh, morning, at the brown brink eastward, springs—
Because the Holy Ghost over the bent
World broods with warm breast and with ah! bright wings
                                                            (31).

Not much of a narrative here, is there? Rather a statement of faith if it was not for the *Oh*, and the *ah*.

  Here are some plain statements that apparently
show no affinity whatsoever with any narrative:

. . . This piece-bright paling shuts the spouse
Christ home, Christ and his mother and all his hallows (32).

  . . . We, life's pride and cared-for crown,
    Have lost that cheer and charm of earth's past prime:
Our make and making break, are breaking, down
To man's last dust, drain fast towards man's first slime
                                                            (35).

Christ minds: Christ's interest, what to avow or amend
    There, éyes them, heart wánts, care haúnts, foot
      fóllows kínd, (40).

Recorded only, I have put my lips on pleas
Would brandle adamantine heaven with ride and jar, did
      Prayer go disregarded (48).

Not that hell knows redeeming,
But for souls sunk in seeming
Fresh, till doomfire burn all,
Prayer shall fetch pity eternal (41).

It now begins to look as if, far from writing narrative poetry, Hopkins was intent on writing religious poetry, and that he misused narrative poetry to make his religious point. This would imply an inexcusable clash with his insistence that first and foremost poetry must show seriousness, integrity, honesty to oneself.

The difficulty to which we just now have given our attention is in reality something precious, as it opens heart and mind, thought and vision, joy and pain of the poet. When a child narrates, tells the story of what happened at school, at a ballgame or whatever, wherever, the story does not end when the event or incident has been communicated. At the end there is surprise, or admiration, or darkness. We are familiar with this, the child asking: can you understand this? is this not unbelievable? or ridiculous? or very sad? Have you ever heard or seen such a thing? Or you should have seen the blood, you should have heard the scream, and so forth. Part of the story-telling is the reaction of the person who is telling the story; he is not just communicating an event. The child is evidently involved; he is not just an outsider or a spectator. He reacts, but not in the categories of cause and effect, or of motive and action. But, then, it is only to be expected and only very human that Hopkins's narrative poems, if they are truly narrative, will always contain his reaction, as an essential part of a well-told story.

There is far more in Hopkins's case. It is not merely that he cannot resist telling us about apparently *significant events*, such as a hawk in flight on an early morning, or the sight of a soldier, or the death of a blacksmith who was his parishioner, or a skylark in its cage, or a somewhat mysterious light that moves in the dark, or a light behind a window (resp. 36, 63, 53, 39, 40, 46), but apparently *insignificant details* also hold his attention and are woven into the story. Nothing escapes his penetrating awareness. This is precisely what we should expect because a child is given to the same weakness, if we might call it that. A child will "embellish" his story, or, rather, give it deeper meaning by mentioning "you should have seen that dog, huge frightening eyes, even more frightening teeth, and a tail . . . ," or "and the way she said it, you would think she was God herself, her feet like copper, her body like cement. . . . "

When a child brings into his story so very many details that could be readily dispensed with, that is, according to adult reckoning, is it really unthinkable that the child is inscaping reality? Inscape does this: nothing is irrelevant, every facet is precious. The child and Hopkins meet, and to me it is of the utmost importance to try to understand this. Consequently, there was no way out for Hopkins but to tell us *where* the Deutschland was wrecked, *why* there were five nuns and not six or four, *why* the tall nun spoke in this way, *why* they happened to be Franciscan nuns, *why* it happened on the seventh of December, and so on. There was no way out for Hopkins but to tell us about Marcus, high her captain, about Bristol where Sydney Fletcher was born, why Carisbrook, and Appledurcombe, and Ventnor, and Boniface Down are so much a part of the country he loved. There was no way out for the poet as story-teller but to talk about Sydney's mother and his sweetheart. Again, there was no way out for Hopkins but to tell us all about God's Grandeur and to observe how all is seared, bleared, smeared, smudged. One might call *Spring* a typical example of nature poetry. For those who know how to listen, it is narrative poetry which finds its ending in an appeal to Christ to cherish and protect "all this juice and all this joy" (33). It is not a matter of Hopkins's *describing* what struck him; but when he mentions the weeds, a bird's eggs, a thrush's singing, the blue heavens, the little lambs, it is the child, lost in so much richness and beauty, impatient to tell us not that there were lambs, but that they were jumping around, and that his ears tingled because of the bird's song, and so forth. A well-nigh classic example is given in *The Windhover*. He tells us about the falcon in flight, but the heart of the *story* is given in the line about which a good deal has been written by scholars who often lack the attitude and the vision of a child:

Brute beauty and valour and act, oh, air, pride, plume, here
    Buckle! (36).

I do not think that the word *buckle* would cause any great difficulty to a child. He might feel inclined to place all those nouns one below the other and then wonder how they buckle together into an inseparable whole.

    Is what I have said merely interesting, or is it of importance, perhaps even of paramount importance in order that one might understand, appreciate, and love poem and poet properly, as he deserves? Few will dispute that there is a profound difference between reading an account of the life of Gladstone or Winston Churchill or whomever and listening to the true story well told of their lives, be it in the form of an historical novel, a play, or even a film. In the former case it is, we repeat the word, *information* that dominates with its appeal to gaining knowledge; in the latter, as we pointed out before, its

35

appeal is to the whole person, who now being involved, shares the life in all its colors with the person whose life story he now absorbs. Similarly, whether we approach and *read* the majority of Hopkins's poems as stories or as description of nature or even of his own experiences makes all the difference in the world. We only truly understand and deeply enjoy Hopkins when we are aware that we are dealing with, in most cases, narrative poetry, and learn to *listen* as a child. This is the shocking paradox, that anyone who takes in hand the difficult poetry of Hopkins must not be the intellectual, but must become the child, and in doing so many so-called oddities and obscurities will explode into clarity. After all, what makes adults laugh, what adults think is odd, strange, even ridiculous and not to be taken seriously, is to a child a dreadfully serious matter, precious beyond words, wonderfully beautiful. The remarkable thing is that more often than not the child is right. Surely, it is slightly ridiculous for a grown-up person to be bothered about a lantern moving in the dark; to a child it is unspeakably fascinating, and it makes him wonder "who goes there, where from, and bound where" (40).

One more point. When a child tells us all about a dog, a storm, a quarrel, an accident, what happened in school, or church, or a playground, or the city square, sooner or later he starts to stammer: he cannot find the words that do justice to his story, and to the *inscape* of what he saw and heard. The reason is that there was never a dog like this one... , for he is *inscaping* what presents itself to his senses. Groping for words, he will have recourse to compounds: you know it was a *catdog*, you know the fellow *cryscreamed*, and he may even coin new words: no, it was not green, it was not blue, but some

kind of *bleen*. We find ourselves with the almost ungrasp-
able combination of poet-child-inscape that Hopkins
was.

"Curiouser and curiouser" I am inclined to say with
little Alice. I am also reminded of quite a different adage:
omne nimium vertit in vitium, which means, any too-much
turns into a defect, a vice. We must not go overboard and
now assume that every poem of Hopkins's is narrative
poetry. It would be just as silly as to assume that a child
only tells stories and never comes home badly hurt because of what the teacher said or did or because he
proved to be no good at math. To designate the so-called
terrible sonnets as narrative poetry is untenable, although I gain in understanding and appreciating them if
I remain sensitive to a possible, even likely element of
narrative hidden beyond the cry and the pain.

To close where I began: "On Saturday sailed from
Bremen. . . . " It is not an Oxford scholar, a philosopher
and theologian, learned, let alone a sophisticated person
who writes in this fashion. It is a simple, repeat, simple
human being who wants everyone to know that terrible
things happened, when he was far "away in the loveable
west, on a pastoral forehead of Wales, under a roof and at
rest," and with him so many other good people right
across the country, and those "two hundred souls in the
round, the prey of the gales" (D. 24, 12). And it teaches all
of us much about Hopkins's inscape. Inscaping *The Wreck
of the Deutschland* could never be restricted to what actually took place at sea, as if there were no England and
Wales. To put it bluntly: once inscaped, the shipwreck
was everybody's business, and man's indifference ("The
beholder wanting," "the inmate does not correspond")
only enhances for Hopkins the tragedy and the pain.

three

"my aspens dear. . ."

Hopkins appears to be a heart-broken man when he wrote his *Binsey Poplars* (43). The poem is a lament and "felled 1879" sounds like an epitaph. In our culture lamentation is considered to be unmanly. Pain has to be borne with a "stiff upper lip," and man has to carry on with his life. The situation is much worse when a man grieves, not because his wife or his child or a very good friend has died but because trees were cut down. If he were angry, we would understand; if he were indignant, again we would understand. Besides, to refer to the trees as *my aspens dear* sounds strange, sentimental, most unusual, childlike if not downright childish. When, however, I feel impelled to use these and similar adjectives, I might just touch the very essence of reality, that is, inscape, followed by its powerful, almost shattering instress. It might be that the simple lamentation breaks open the heart of the poet for all to see and understand.

Elsewhere we hear the same sadness gently touching the reader who knows how to listen, his ears wide open:

EARTH, sweet Earth, sweet landscape, with leavès throng

. . . .

That canst but only be, but dost that long—

. . . .

To thriftless reave both our rich round world bare
And none reck of world after, this bids wear
Earth brows of such care, care and dear concern.(58).

It should escape no one's attention how throughout this poem earth is written with a capital E, how only the personal possessive pronouns *Thou* and *Thy* are used; the choice of *sweet, lovely, dear, care, concern* point to the instress of Ribblesdale inscaped by the poet.

There is sadness and anger when Oxford is irreparably damaged:

TOWERY city and branchy between towers;
Cuckoo-echoing, bell-swarmèd, lark-charmèd,
rook-racked, river-rounded;

. . . .

Thou hast a base and brickish skirt there, sours
That neighbour-nature thy grey beauty is grounded
Best in; graceless growth, thou hast confounded
Rural rural keeping—folk, flocks, and flowers (44).

40

Notice once again the use of the pronoun.

Hopkins's joy at watching the sea and off land a skylark, and listening "on ear and ear two noises too old to end" is cruelly disturbed when he painfully observes how "these two shame this shallow and frail town!"

How ring right out our sordid turbid time,
Being pure! We, life's pride and cared-for crown,

Have lost that cheer and charm of earth's past prime ...
(35).

There is an almost homely poem about a house in the valley of the Elwy (34). The poet is overwhelmed by the warm hospitality, a "cordial air":

Lovely the woods, waters, meadows, combes, vales
All the air things wear that build this world of Wales

and then the collapse:

Only the inmate does not correspond ...

The grief and sorrow expressed here and elsewhere are evidently the pain of a man of love, better, a man in love. There is a danger that one takes my aspens *dear* as emotional ornamentation. It is not. Neither is the repeated *sweet* when he addressed the Earth in his Ribblesdale poem (58). Hopkins was far too sensitive to words, had far too great a respect for words to ever use them in any slovenly irresponsible manner. A few lines above we came across *lovely* as joined to woods, waters, meadows, combes, vales of Wales. It does not mean to Hopkins simply attractive or beautiful; it means *loveable*, which implies that he is in love with the waters, and woods, and vales of Wales. Hence, it should not come as a surprise, let

41

alone as a sentimental gesture, that he *kisses his hand* to the stars, *lovely*-asunder starlight (D. 5). Hopkins thought that *The Windhover* was "the best thing he ever wrote": that is the reason why some five years after he wrote the poem he dedicated it to Christ our Lord (36). The wording of the poem is evidence of the poet whose "heart in hiding stirred for a bird," who then could not resist addressing the bird as his *chevalier*, and let his deep love express itself in an "ah, my dear." Not surprisingly we find an *oh* and an O, and that *lovely* in the comparative occurs is now only natural:

> AND the fire that breaks from thee then, a billion
> Times told lovelier, more dangerous, O my chevalier!

Once again the personal pronoun *thee* is used. (Incidentally, Hopkins wrote *told*, but elsewhere we proved he heard *tolled* as well.) To us mortals, *lovely* has lost a good deal of its original meaning, but Hopkins inscaped the words he used, and their instress struck him. There is "hurrahing in harvest," hurrahing because of the "*lovely* behaviour of silk-sack clouds!" and in the end the poet is bewildered and grieved because no eyes, no looks, no lips ever gave the Savior "a rapturous love's greeting of realer, of rounder replies" (38). To some it will seem farfetched to link *lovely* with *rapturous love* some six lines further on. To Hopkins it was spontaneous, inescapable. No wonder then that, when he addresses "Earth, sweet Earth, sweet landscape," he writes of "Thy lovely dale,"; one should sense the deep respect as indicated, once again, by the use of *thou* and *thy*.

Hopkins's choice of *dear* and *lovely* is very relevant to the implications of inscaping and instressing. We should not miss in this connection his predilection for the adjec-

42

tive *sweet*. Not merely in the poem *Ribblesdale*, but also in the exuberance of his story about *Spring*; "the weeds shoot long and *lovely* and lush," and in the sestet he asks himself

> What is all this juice and all this joy?

and gives the answer

> A strain of the earth's *sweet* being in the beginning
> In Eden garden

(where we do well to recall that *strain* here also stands for melody).

Just now we used the word *exuberance*, the reason being that at times his love cannot be restrained. In *The Starlight Night* (32) (remember: I kiss my hand to the *lovely*-asunder starlight, D. 5), we find eight exclamation marks in the octet, and another five in the sestet of this sonnet. But even without such clear marks of love, we sense its presence in the occasional poem *Inversnaid*:

> What would the world be, once bereft
> Of wet and of wildness? Let them be left
> O let them be left, wildness and wet;
> Long live the weeds and the wilderness yet (56).

Finally, this love is not blind; it is gentle and honest:

> Nature, bad, base, and blind,
> Dearly thou canst be kind;
> There dearly thén, deárly,
> Dearly thou canst be kind (54).

Indeed, *dearly*, and four times in three short lines.

My *aspens* dear, but more poignant is "rare-dear Britain" (D. 35).

43

> England, whose honour O all my heart woos, wife
> To my creating thought (66),

where *woos* and *wife* are indicative of a very profound love. England here does not stand for a piece of land surrounded by water, but for people, for *dear and dogged man* (58). His deep and honest love for his fellow man shines through in simple poems like *Spring and Fall* (55), *The Handsome Heart* (47), and *At the Wedding March* (52). I sense the love and the terrible pain when his conversion proves to be more than his parents can handle. He writes of "father and mother *dear*," and this some twenty years after he left the Anglican Communion. When he helps a blacksmith in his last days and hours, it is again a man of and in love who writes:

> This seeing the sick *endears* them to us, us too it *endears*
> (53).

He is pretty matter-of-fact about the soldier, "the greater part, but frail clay, nay but foul clay," and yet, seeing the redcoat, and "calling the calling manly ... it *dears* the artist after his art" (63). And time is no obstacle "so *dear* to me, so arch-especial a spirit as heaves in Henry Purcell" (45; notice the present tense).

His love is genuine, so genuine that he is not ashamed of his tears for the drowned sailors and travellers "comfortless unconfessed" (D. 31). His love for the victim in *The Loss of the Eurydice*, Sydney Fletcher, embraces his mother, wife, or his sweetheart. Here as in *The Wreck of the Deutschland* the poet is touched "in his bower of bone" (D. 18). His love for and compassion with the five sisters make him cry, to his own astonishment, and so he seeks an explanation of his tears:

>   Ah, touched in your bower of bone,
>   Are you! turned for an exquisite smart,
>   Have you! . . .

. . . .

Why, tears! is it? tears; such a melting, a madrigal start! (D. 18).

It was a matter of "tears sad true love should shed," here as it was when he somehow tried to comfort the mother, wife, or sweetheart of Sydney:

>   O well wept, mother have lost son;
>   Wept, wife; wept, sweetheart would be one:
>   Though grief yield them no good
>   Yet shed what tears sad truelove should (L. 105-108).

The disappointment, pain, love of *My aspens dear* kept his very being intact until the end. Hopkins was evidently tempted to lose his *self*, to become the pessimist, to give in to despair, which he calls *Carrion Comfort* (64). There remains alive in him, no matter how alone, how lonely, how much the stranger in this world, his ability to "kind *love* both give and get" (66).

Does what we have written in this chapter not clearly show that Hopkins is a typically romantic poet, perhaps with a more burning sense of beauty, a greater intensity of living, but fundamentally belonging to the school of romantics of the beginning of the nineteenth century as well as to that of the romantics of his own Oxford days and later? I do not think that any person, aware of, attuned to the inscape and instress of whatever is perceived by the senses, of whatever is experienced in dealings with fellow men in the world around him, could possibly become a romantic. The reason is that romanticism is by itself restrictive: it does not open itself fully to

inscape and instress; it puts up certain barriers; it is
sensitive to certain aspects of reality, to certain perfections. Hopkins was just too great for this. We should not
fall back upon his being a Christian, a very religious
person, a priest, to explain the difference. Just listen:

Our law says: Love what are | love's worthiest, were all known;
World's loveliest—men's selves. Self | flashes off frame and
    face (62).

This is the reason why Hopkins was a man in love, and
hence a man in pain. Men's selves are most worthy of
love, although he knew too much of man's malice dogged
in den (D. 9), of man's smudge (31), of the blindness of
the beholder (38), of the indifference of the inmate (34).
When he tries to discern why he loves Purcell "so dear to
me," he discovers:

    Not mood in him nor meaning, proud fire or sacred fear,
    Or love or pity or all that sweet notes not his might nursle:
    It is the forgèd feature finds me; it is the rehearsal
Of own, of abrúpt sélf there so thrusts on, so throngs the ear
                                (45).

Beyond the words and beyond the melody and beyond all
the sweet notes, Hopkins inscapes the self, this to such an
extent that the instress can be expressed only by a self
that is, notice, abrupt (translation: which hits him), that
thrusts itself on the ear, that throngs the ear: inescapable,
powerfully alive. He then drives home how his love now
forces him only to "have an eye to the sakes of Purcell,
quaint moonmarks, to his pelted plumage under wings"
(45).

    When Hopkins had arrived at inscape, he knew him-
self in the presence of a self, no matter whether he

inscaped a tree, or a star, or a brick. Nothing was any longer a lifeless, selfless thing. Lifeless, not in the biological sense, but

> Each mortal thing does one thing and the same:
>   Deals out that being indoors each one dwells;
>   Selves—goes itself; *myself* it speaks and spells,
> Crying *What I do is me: for that I came.*(57).

We see this love for any self break through when, almost logically, he addresses the earth, "that has no tongue to plead, no heart to feel" and yet

> That canst but only be, but dost that long—
>
> Thou canst but be, but that thou well dost; strong
> Thy plea with him who dealt, nay does now deal,
> Thy lovely dale down thus ... (58).

"World's loveliest," indeed, men's selves, but it implies that every *self* is lovely, precious, alive. It is then not at all surprising that Hopkins can only see his "sweet earth" as filled with unique selves, and hence as charged with the Grandeur of God which

> ... will flame out, like shining from shook foil;
> It gathers to a greatness, like the ooze of oil
> Crushed (31).

Pied Beauty is very short and simple compared with the majestic *The Wreck of the Deutschland*. It strikes us as a little child in a family of grown-up brothers and sisters; it is sheer wonder at beauty so rich and so varied:

> All things counter, original, spare, strange;
>   Whatever is fickle, freckled (who knows how?)
>   With swift, slow; sweet, sour; adazzle, dim;

and then the penetrating vision:

> He fathers-forth whose beauty is past change:
> Praise him (37).

I called the poem *In the Valley of the Elwy* unpretentious, and no wonder when it opens in this way:

> I REMEMBER a house where all were good
>   To me, God knows, deserving no such thing:
>   Comforting smell breathed at very entering,
> Fetched fresh, as I suppose, off some sweet wood (34).

He then moves from "these kind people" to the observation: it is so typically Wales. This is followed by a regretful "only the inmate does not correspond." Hopkins might have left it at that, but he could not. Everything is brimful of life while he inscapes and instresses this world of Wales, the exception being man, and hence there surges within him the yearning expressed in the prayer:

> God, lover of souls, swaying considerate scales,
> Complete thy creature dear O where it fails,
>   Being mighty a master, being a father and fond (34).

One does well here to pay careful attention to *complete* and *dear*: the self is so dear, that is, precious, but must not remain maimed, incomplete.

One might deduce from these four illustrations (*Ribblesdale, The Wreck of the Deutschland, Pied Beauty, In the Valley of the Elwy*) that Hopkins is a religious poet. I do not think that this is a correct conclusion. I do not even call him a nature poet. It is really a simple matter: where the poet, whatever way he turns, sees the brook or the river, there is no way for him but to be aware of the source. In *To what serves Mortal Beauty?* (62) one can trace the brook, the river, and the source. Hopkins mentions that mortal beauty, although it might be dangerous, "keeps warm men's wits to the things that are, to what good means," where just a glance may achieve more than a penetrating concentrated vision. This is the brook. He then turns to men's inner beauty, to love's worthiest, world's loveliest, men's selves; it is the river. Wonderful as this is, it is so because it is "heaven's sweet gift," with all the echoes of "He fathers-forth." Here is the source, "God's better beauty, grace." Inscape, instress, sakes, self are marked by grace, this in the twofold sense of graciousness and of God-at-work. One probably understands better the strong urge always "to flash from the flame to the flame, tower from the grace to the grace" (D. 3).

Because of its importance I pursue this topic a little further. Sometimes a lantern moves along the night, and Hopkins is interested: who goes there? where from and bound to where? The person disappears in the dark, and regretfully out of sight is out of mind. Not so. The unknown fleeting *self* is far too precious "to be consumed by death or distance," and, if once again I may use the illustration of river and source, Hopkins reaches out to the source: Christ minds, first, fast friend (40).

Hopkins—this man of love—was shaken by the death of five nuns, victims of the unjust laws in Bismarck's Germany. However, the astonishing thing is that he cries not because of the five sisters, but because of "a fourth the doom to be drowned" (D. 12). These victims of the shipwreck were not just unfortunate sailors and passengers. Their selves are so much more: comfortless, unconfessed (D. 31). But then the full impact of instress breaks through: "no not uncomforted." Part of the poet's vision and experience remains: "He fathers-forth whose beauty is past change." He now writes of "lovely-felicitous Providence, finger of a tender of, O of a feathery delicacy" and of "the master of the tides . . . throned behind death with a sovereignty that heeds but hides, bodes but abides" (D. 31, 32).

Just as there is something orchestral about the beginning of *Spelt from Sibyl's Leaves*,

> EARNEST, earthless, equal, attuneable, | vaulty, voluminous . . . stupendous
> Evening strains to be tíme's vást, | womb-of-all, home-of-all, hearse-of-all night (61),

so we find the violins, the flutes, the trumpets, and the drums in *That Nature is a Heraclitean Fire and of the comfort of the Resurrection* (72). Yet this very impressive poem is really *My aspens dear* on a larger scale. It illustrates what I said about the brook, the river, and the source, except that in this poem the brook is a torrent, and the river threatens to burst its banks. Hopkins speaks of nature's bonfire, still burning on, and then moves on to nature's "bonniest, dearest to her, her clearest-selvèd spark, man." (Incidentally, do not miss the adjective *dearest*, and the superlative *clearest-selvèd* implies that there are in nature many less-clearly-selved sparks.) It is a matter of "manshape, that shone sheer off, disseveral, a star." Here too, the beholder, the inmate is failing. But completely in harmony with the conviction and vision is *God's Grandeur*: any mark of man may be blurred by vastness and beaten level by time and even blotted out by death, but "there lives the deepest freshness deep down things . . . because the Holy Ghost over the bent world broods" (31). Now it is a heart's-clarion (with the hyphen!); it is a beacon shining across man's foundering deck; a potsherd turns into immortal diamond: The Resurrection.

Indeed, it is understandable how after these examples—and many more of Hopkins's poems end on a "pious tone"—readers conclude that Hopkins is a religious poet, and that he was a religious poet because he was a religious and a priest, with the implication that it was his duty and vocation to be pious, to set a good example, to edify, and to write in order to bolster the Church. Nothing is further from the truth. That is why the controversy about the poet and the priest is rooted in a false perspective.

Hopkins is not a romantic poet, nor is he a nature poet, nor is he a religious poet, as should be clear from this chapter. What then? Hopkins is the poet he is because he was—and I knowingly use the word—so *terribly* human, a man of love, a man in love with whatever is, as always, fathered by God; and hence a man well acquainted with the disappointments and pain, and hence "of realty the rarest-veinèd unraveller" as Scotus was. We should prefer *see-er* to *unraveller*, but Hopkins adds when speaking of Scotus "a not rivalled insight," so applicable to himself. My aspens dear. . . .

To those who are acquainted with the *Spiritual Exercises* of St. Ignatius Loyola, the above will probably not come unexpected. These people will point out that Hopkins was not merely familiar with the contemplation to attain divine love, in which the retreatant is asked to see how all goodness and beauty descend from God, all-good, all-beautiful, but that Hopkins had reached such depth of spiritual life that he shared this vision of Ignatius. Moreover, they will point out that Hopkins had really come to share the vision of God's Son Himself,

51

wherein nature becomes so transparent to Him that he sees that it is the Father who takes care of the sparrows and clothes the lilies (Luke 12). The key word of Ignatius is *de arriba*, that is, all things proceed *from above*. Now, Hopkins subscribes to this: "He fathers-forth whose beauty is past change." But there is a significant difference. The *de arriba* is an article of faith, and hence every *self* must be precious. But the *de arriba* may also be an inescapable conclusion to which the inscape of whatever is leads. With Hopkins it is not faith that leads to the preciousness of self, to inscape; it is the other way around. It is the perception and experience of instress and inscape that drive him to "He fathers-forth. . . . " It is because the poet was too intensely and uncontaminatedly human that he not only came "God to aggrandise, God to glorify," but was "a-wanting . . . the eagerer a-wanting Jessy or Jack . . . God to aggrándise, God to glorify" (46).

It began with *My aspens dear*, and it ended with "Be adored among men" (D. 9). Once again, I find it difficult to see Hopkins as primarily a religious poet. With a startling paradox: he is too human for that; but just because he was so intensely human, he gained an all-embracing vision of God. There is more to aspens dear than just their *haecceitas*.

I have a strong suspicion, not to say conviction, that it is this human-ness that endears him to me, and to many others.

four

"*pitched past pitch of grief. . .*"

In previous chapters I could see Hopkins on the one hand simple as a child; on the other, so intensively human that he was a man of love, in love, and, hence, unavoidably a man acquainted with pain. Because the *selves*, all *selves*, once inscaped and instressed, were so wonderfully unique and precious, he could only grieve when they were damaged in the many ways man managed to do them harm: by indifference, by smearing and smudging them, by hiding them behind sour bricks, and so on. However, when readers of Hopkins's poetry find themselves confronted with words like *terrible* and *terror* (respectively 64 and D. 2), they have to face a totally different world of sufferings. They have to wrestle with the first eleven stanzas of *The Wreck of the Deutschland*, and with the so-called terrible sonnets (64, 65, 66, 67, 69, and 74), to which might be added his last sonnet written about a month before he died, in which a certain resignation alleviates the terror or the pain.

All these poems enjoy, if that is the right word, a certain notoriety. But at a first reading the notoriety of *The Wreck of the Deutschland* is different from that accorded to the terrible sonnets. Certainly, there is the riddle of pain in all of them, but the notoriety of the former is to a very large extent explained by the oddities, the obscurities, the license in the use of language, the disregard of grammar and syntax, some outrageous rhymes, and so forth—a somewhat willful break with traditional poetry. The notoriety, however, that has befallen the sonnets from Hopkins's years in Dublin proceeds for many from an assumed, possibly real, conflict between the poet and the Jesuit priest. Words like *neurotic* and *psychotic* have been used to explain the terror of these later poems.

Indeed, I have asked myself many a time, in order to come to an understanding of Hopkins as a human being, as a priest, and as a poet, how he could possibly write

> No worst, there is none. Pitched past pitch of grief,
> More pangs will, schooled at forepangs, wilder wring (65).

What bitter suffering prompted him to cry out

> Not, I'll not, carrion comfort, Despair, not feast on
>   thee;
> Not untwist—slack they may be—these last strands of man
>   In me ór, most weary, cry *I can no more* (64)?

What has happened to a man who in cold blood complains to his God

> Why do sinners' ways prosper? and why must
> Disappointment all I endeavour end? (74)?

or just as cold-bloodedly observes

> I see
> The lost are like this, and their scourge to be
> As I am mine, their sweating selves; but worse (67)

or states in a matter-of-fact way

> I cast for comfort I can no more get
> By groping round my comfortless, than blind
> Eyes in their dark can day or thirst can find
> Thirst's all-in-all in all a world of wet (69)?

There is surely something somewhere wrong when a priest and poet is so presumptuous, and evidently angry, even arrogant, as to throw into God's face words like

> But ah, but O thou terrible, why wouldst thou rude on me
> Thy wring-world right foot rock? lay a lionlimb against
>   me? scan
> With darksome devouring eyes my bruisèd bones? (64).

Whether such lines are typical of a neurotic person is a legitimate question, or whether they are lines of a schizophrenic, where the split here is between a poet yearning for wings of freedom and a priest locked in a harness of unpalatable duties. In this case there would be plenty of reason for compassion, but not for friendship.

But there was, long before the pain of the Dublin sonnets, the sufferings of *The Wreck of the Deutschland*, where the word *terrible* is not used but where we are

startled by the noun *terror*, and it is Christ's terror. In the
second stanza Hopkins confesses:

> I did say yes
> O at lightning and lashed rod;
> Thou heardst me truer than tongue confess
> Thy terror, O Christ, O God

and in the same stanza he writes of "the swoon of a heart
that the sweep and the hurl of thee trod hard down with a
horror of height." The stanza that follows has:

> The frown of his face
> Before me, the hurtle of hell
> Behind, where, where was a, where was a place?

In the opening stanza it is fear:

> Thou hast bound bones and veins in me, fastened me flesh,
> And after it almost unmade, what with dread,
> Thy doing: and dost thou touch me afresh?

Hopkins writes of the "rebel, man's malice, wrung with
wrecking and storm" (D. 9; notice that the verb *to wring* is
also found in the line from 64 quoted above). Life is a
matter of "waving with the meadow," and then forgetting
that "there must the sour scythe cringe, and the blear
share come" (D. 11; yes, he wrote *share*; why not *shear*?
Because it is already strongly suggested by the scythe,
and almost a homonym of *share*).

Now, when I wrote about his aspens dear, I had
occasion to point out that this man of love, and in love,
was also familiar with pain. Many a time this pain was
somehow linked with God: either because the beholder
was wanting (38), or because the inmate did not correspond (34), or because the sailors went to their death

"comfortless unconfessed," and his "rare-dear Britain"
did not know her hour of grace (L. 85-104). The joy he
experienced in inscaping and instressing whatever was
alive (and to Hopkins *life* does not stand only for biological life: just read *Pied Beauty* again) was always somewhat
mellowed by his sharp experience that no self—above all
"world's loveliest—men's selves" (62) and "nature's bonniest, dearest to her, her clearest-selvèd spark man"—
ever showed the fullness of its beauty, of its grandeur.
Often, almost always, that last glistening spark, "God's
better beauty, grace" was lacking. We do well to remember again that grace is here not only used in the
theological sense but in the meaning of *graciousness*; and
this *graciousness* is in Hopkins's vision always the splendor
of the Father, or, if it is preferred, a spark of God's
Grandeur. It hurt him, it caused him grief, not, we repeat, just as a Christian but as a great human being with
the simplicity of a child.

It should be clear to anyone that this pain would
never be described as a horror of height or as being
lashed with a rod, nor would this pain remind him of
being struck by lightning, or as threatened by the hurtle
of hell (all phrases taken from *The Wreck of the Deutschland*). We now move in a different world of sufferings; we
now are with a different Hopkins. Scholars have given
various explanations for this change from the harshness
of the opening stanzas of *The Wreck of the Deutschland* to a
milder sadness that marks the poems written between
1878 and his departure to Dublin, some six years later.
Fatigue is mentioned; disappointment and frustration;
the unbearable tension between the poet and one who
felt himself hemmed in by his duties as a religious and a
priest in formation; the yoke of life according to the vows

of poverty, chastity, and obedience and its unavoidable clash with an over-sensitive man who wished to breathe the freedom of nature around him. Depression is supposed to have played its part, which was only partially relieved by his enthusiasm about the discovery of Scotus. Many other causes are given that account for the painful writing of the introduction to *The Wreck of the Deutschland*.

I am willing to admit that there is some truth in what scholars bring to the fore, but then is all this, *mutatis mutandis*, not part of any person's life? Is there a happily married couple that does not, at some time or other, have to wrestle with disappointment, worry, boredom, lack of freedom, even a trace of depression, misunderstanding, and so on? There is one source of suffering which is mentioned by Hopkins himself and all too frequently passed over by critics. When withdrawing for some eight days to be spent in prayer, he wrote that he understood how asking to be raised to a higher degree of grace was also asking to be lifted on a higher cross. This understanding came to him when he was meditating on the Crucifixion. Indeed, he wrote this in 1883. But to a spiritually mature man such understanding does not come as a sudden unexpected revelation. Hopkins had been aware of this reality for many, many years because it is at the heart of the *Spiritual Exercises* of Ignatius; in fact, it is at the heart of being a Christian, and we find this conviction expressed in the second part of *The Wreck of the Deutschland*.

The second part of the poem I can read only as written first, before the opening twelve stanzas. The hint of his rector that someone might write a poem about the shipwreck in which many people, among them five German Franciscan nuns, were drowned was for Hopkins a most unexpected invitation to break his self-imposed poetic silence. Does this imply that one morning or evening around mid-December in 1875 he sat down, in the second year of his theological studies, and wrote "THOU mastering me God"? The details given in the poem are evidence enough that he not only read the newspaper accounts but made himself familiar with the when, the how, the where, the who, and so on. Moreover, Hopkins could never accept the tragedy as objectively stated and reported: a man of inscape and instress cannot possibly be a spectator, an outsider. Hence, I cannot but conclude that there was first the inscape and instress of the shipwreck, and that, once he began to write, he rendered what had happened, not as read in the papers, but as profoundly experienced, inscaped, and instressed by him.

To me this has always been a blessed discovery. The second part was written first, and in writing the second part, his own self opened up and showed unexpected depths of the mystery of both being and suffering. Consequently, I, for one, became aware that I could understand Hopkins and his poetry and his sufferings only when I deeply penetrated the *story* of the Deutschland's shipwreck as narrated in the second part. Why is this important? What is its result?

Very obviously, the poem is not about the wreck of a ship—it is not about a poet's sufferings. But equally obvious is that *Deutschland* does not stand for a country, nor even for a ship; it stands, right from the very start, for "take settler and seamen, tell men with women, two hundred souls in the round." *Deutschland* stands for people, and

O Father, not under thy feathers nor ever as guessing
The goal was a shoal, of a fourth the doom to be drowned
(12)

Consequently, from the very beginning the sea is not frightening waves but "widow-making unchilding unfathering deeps" (D. 13). The theme is not a shipwreck, but it .is human sufferings. Not just human sufferings, but the problem of man's sufferings, now shared by Hopkins as a fellow man, and hence crying or praying:

> Yet did the dark side of the bay of thy blessing
> Not vault them, the million of rounds of thy mercy not
> reeve even them in? (12).

The theme throughout remains the people:

> To the shrouds they took,–they shook in the hurling and
> horrible airs (15).

This is the fifteenth stanza. The sixteenth is all about a brave sailor who was pitched to his death at a blow. In the seventeenth stanza, the people are fighting the cold and the waves, the women are wailing, the children are crying, and a sister towers like a prophetess in the tumult. At this point it is remarkable that Hopkins is himself surprised that he is "touched in his bower of bone," that he is close to tears and wonders why this is (D. 18). Most noteworthy, because these tears have nothing to do with fatigue, frustration, or other sources mentioned to explain the poet's sufferings.

Hopkins continues his narrative; but more than ever before, it is people that concern him. The five stanzas that follow give us the inscape of that tall sister who like "a lioness arose breasting the babble" (D. 17). It is as if in the twenty-fourth stanza Hopkins has regained his composure:

> Away in the loveable west
> On a pastoral forehead of Wales,

> I was under a roof here, I was at rest,
>> And they the prey of the gales (24).

One might almost expect the poem to end here and leave the reader with the painful contrast between the drowning sisters and a young theologian with a roof over his head, and at rest (notice, for future reference, this "at rest"). Except for one thing: inscaping the tall courageous sister could not possibly imply complete deafness to what the sister was saying; and as the word proceeds from the abundance of the heart, inscape would now lead the way to instress

> She to the black-about air, to the breaker . . .
> . . . .
>> Was calling 'O Christ, Christ, come quickly'

which is followed by "what did she mean?" The five stanzas that follow are Hopkins's effort truly and deeply to instress this sister. There is an unmistakable passion to pierce through the words spoken by the sister, and in the end (D. 29) the answer is none other than the one suggested at the beginning:

> The cross to her she calls Christ to her, christens her
>> wild-worst
>>> Best.

Here we find the inscape and instress of the sister coming together in the unmeasurably profound "she christens her wild-worst Best." Her wild-worst, that is, her sudden, early death in the cold wintry waters of the North Sea. And she calls it not the best thing that ever happened to her, but she gave the wild-worst a name (christens!), and the name is *Best*, with a capital. This is crucial in understanding Hopkins here and elsewhere where the instress and inscape of the wild widow-making, unchilding un-fathering deeps are experienced as if they were a person, a person whose name is *Best*, none better. It is exactly the same as what precedes immediately

> The cross to her she calls Christ to her ...

The poem should have ended here, with the echoes of the words of St. Paul: death, where is your sting; death is dead (1 Cor. 15). Those well acquainted with Hopkins's poetry will almost involuntarily be reminded of a much later poem,

> Across my foundering deck shone
> A beacon, an eternal beam (72)

in which the beacon and the beam refer to the Resurrec-tion, the victory of life over death.

However, it is so typical of Hopkins that the poem could not end here; true enough,

> she has thee for the pain, for the
> Patience;

and then, with tears in his eyes and a bleeding heart:

> but pity of the rest of them!
> . . . .

Comfortless unconfessed of them— (D. 31).

The correction follows: "No not uncomforted"! Here too Hopkins finds the traces of the wild-worst given the name *Best*, through a delicate, a feathery delicacy with which

> past all
> Grasp God, throned behind

Death with a sovereignty that heeds but hides, bodes but
abides; (D. 32)

and this

> With a mercy that outrides
> The all of water, an ark ... (D. 33)

comforts all. This is not a return to the inscape of the
crew and passengers (stanzas 12-17), but the whole scene
of the terrible tragedy is now instressed and inscaped,
which leads to the awareness, not to say vision, of the
"master of the tides," "The Christ of the Father compas-
sionate" (D. 33). Here is the end of the story of the
wrecked ship, not just because the "jay-blue heavens of
pied and peeled May" were appearing (D. 26), symbol of
the calm after the storm, of the final victory over death.
This victory is mirrored in the two closing stanzas, in
their very rhythm. Prosodically, not a thing has changed.
The shape of the stanzas remains the same, sprung
rhythm is still faithfully adhered to, yet the effect is so
different. A restfulness returns:

> Now burn, new born to the world ...

and then with reference to Christ:

> Not a dooms-day dazzle in his coming nor dark as he
>   came;
> Kind, but royally reclaiming his own;
> A released shower, let flash to the shire, not a lightning of
>   fire hard-hurled (34).

The very wording makes the listener go slowly and makes
him taste the peace now resting upon the once so cruel
waters. It is no surprise that this expressed itself in a

prayer, a prayer which is undoubtedly majestic, yet it is so simple and breathes hope, even a trace of joy:

> Dame, at our door
> Drowned, and among our shoals,
> Remember us in the roads, the heaven-haven of the
> reward:
> Our King back, Oh, upon English souls!
> Let him easter in us ... (D. 35).

Sprung rhythm suggests a deviation from non-sprung rhythm, that is, presumably, from a smooth, regularly recurring beat. Sprung rhythm suggests something like unrest, jerkiness, impatience on the part of the poet, perhaps even a trace of vehemence, of breaking the barriers of normal rhythms. That is where the mastery of Hopkins comes in: in the closing two stanzas above sprung rhythm stands ironically for coming to rest, calm, and peace.

I might have raised the suspicion that I wanted to analyse the poem and show its component parts. Nothing is further from the fact. But I never understood the *sufferings* expressed in the first part of this poem until I had begun reading and listening to the second part; and one result of this is that now I have to italicize the word *suffering*. This forced me to no longer compare or contrast or even link together *The Wreck of the Deutschland* with the terrible sonnets as if the life of Hopkins, poet and Jesuit, showed the pattern of: sufferings—a lull—sufferings. "Pitched past pitch of grief" does *not* refer to the experience expressed in the first part of *The Wreck of the Deutschland*.

To understand this, we must realize that the last line written is not the end of the poetic experience. No poet worth his name writes that last line and considers that that is the end; for one thing, he carries the inspiration and the experience with him for a considerable time to come. In Hopkins's case the situation is the same, but in a far more intense way. "On Saturday sailed from Bremen" is, as I pointed out, the clearest indication that we are dealing with narrative poetry, with a story, which the poet feels urged to tell. Because he is not a reporter, but a storyteller, Hopkins could not but become deeply involved in the story he narrates, and, as we have seen, even unto tears. Now this involvement places beyond any doubt that, when the story had been told, inscape, instress, the self had taken hold of the poet in what I would call a dramatic way. Seriousness, honesty, which he esteemed so highly in any poet, forced him to round off, as it were, the story of the Deutschland by giving expression to his own self. Hence it proved well-nigh impossible for Hopkins not to end the poem by adding a stanza thirty-six, which in actual fact is stanza number one.

> I admire thee, master of the tides,
>   Of the Yore-flood, of the year's fall;
> The recurb and the recovery of the gulf's sides, . . . (D. 32)

and hence the opening lines:

> THOU mastering me
>   God! giver of breath and bread;
> World's strand, sway of the sea . . .

But of far greater consequence, where narration by a poet is concerned, is that when the story is told, very clear indications, to put it mildly, are discernible of the poet identifying himself with the main characters of the story. Because of its importance, I want to make this clear by an

illustration based upon fact. There was a special per-
formance of *Traitor's Gate*, a play by Morna Stuart, in the
late 1930s. When Thomas More is in the Tower of London, he is visited by his favorite daughter Meg; and
tactfully Meg tries to change her father's mind, using the
argument that "all the others," meaning bishops, cour-
tiers, and so forth, had taken the oath. Why was it that at
this painfully harrowing scene suddenly very, very many
spectators got a cold and needed a handkerchief? Without wanting to, they had come to identify themselves so
much with the suffering More that they were near tears.
Such identification is the inspiration of the first part of
the poem. Hence, I cannot read the first stanza except
with full emphasis on the words I now place in italics:

> THOU mastering *me*
> God! giver of breath and bread;
> World's strand, sway of the sea;
> Lord of living and dead;
> Thou hast bound bones and veins in *me*, fastened *me* flesh
> . . . .
>
> . . . and dost thou touch *me* afresh?
> Over again *I* feel thy finger and find thee.

The stanza should recall the eighteenth stanza, where
identification in no way appears to be accidental or inci-
dental:

> "Ah, touched in your bower of bone are you! . . . mother
> of being in me, heart."

In a similar way the pronouns *I* and *me* receive the main
stress in the second stanza:

> I did say yes
> O at lightning and lashed rod;
> Thou heardst me truer than tongue confess
> Thy terror, O Christ, O God.

as they do in the third stanza, until we find exactly the same sufferings expressed in two different ways:

> The cross to her she calls Christ to her, christens her
> wild-worst
> Best (D. 24)

and

> To flash from the flame to the flame then, tower from the
> grace to the grace (D. 3).

Even the calm that followed the night of the shipwreck

> For how to the heart's cheering
> The down-dugged ground-hugged grey
> Hovers off, the jay-blue heavens appearing
> Of pied and peeled May!
> Blue-beating and hoary-glow height; or night, still higher,
> With belled fire and the moth-soft Milky Way, (D. 26)

is experienced in stanza five:

> I kiss my hand
> To the stars, lovely-asunder
> Starlight, wafting him out of it; and
> Glow, glory in thunder;
> Kiss my hand to the dappled-with-damson west:

Hopkins then adds how at the end of the story—beginning harmlessly enough with "On Saturday sailed from Bremen," moving through the tragedy of stanzas fourteen to seventeen, and ending in "a mercy that outrides the all of water, an ark for the listener" (D. 33)—he is faced by a mystery (D. 5), not just the mystery of man's sufferings, but the greater, more incomprehensible mystery of a "lovely-felicitous Providence, finger of a tender of, O of a feathery delicacy" (D. 31); not just the mystery of "Dame, at our door drowned and among our shoals," but the greater mystery of Him who comes "kind, but royally reclaiming his own," "the master of the tides" (D. 35, 32).

I might have given the impression of finding parallel passages and expressions in the two parts of the poems. It was never my intention; but it is almost self-evident that in telling the story of the shipwreck properly, part of his inscaping himself, part of his own *self* is now the tragedy in all its aspects. As we saw, when the waves have calmed down, when the poet addresses God with "I admire thee, master of the tides"(D. 32) and "make mercy in all of us, out of us all mastery, but be adored, but be adored King" (D. 10), the mystery remains. But one does not in a dumb sort of way accept any mystery. There is always "the search for insight," which is the object of faith according to St. Augustine. In the words of Hopkins, "the mystery must be instressed, stressed" (D. 5). And so he goes in search (stanza six and following), and the answer is none other than "the sea [was] flint-flake, black-backed in the regular blow . . . in cursed quarter, the wind" (D. 13), but also "the jay-blue heavens appearing of pied and peeled May" (D. 26), none other than

Thou art lightning and love, I found it, a winter and warm
(D. 9).

In conclusion, I do not think it correct to maintain that the shipwreck was symbolic of Hopkins's own life,

that those seven years as a Jesuit with their poetic silence, .
or those eleven years after his conversion when he became a stranger to many, especially his dear parents,
stood for tragedy, destruction, even some sort of death.
The reason is very obvious why this is untrue: *The Wreck
of the Deutschland* is not a story about a ship in a storm—it
is a story about people and, inescapably, the Master of the
tides. It then takes on through inscape and instress the
dimensions of all people and the Giver of breath and
bread. The story now becomes a true epos.

At the end of the first part of this chapter, I can well
imagine how readers may find it difficult to agree with
my reading of the poem. When all is said, what still
worries them is the almost unbearably painful succession
of lightning, lashed rod, the sweep and the hurl of Christ
that trod hard down his heart with a horror of height;
and the frown of his face before, the hurtle of hell behind
and his very being on fire with stress (D. 2, 3). Surely,
such expressions point to a person "pitched past pitch of
grief," and hence they point to some sort of hellish existence that, once given the chance, broke all silence and
cried out loud of its sufferings. I understand this reaction; it had been my own for many, many years. I make
two observations: (1) existence was not mere sufferings;
there was also the fling of the heart to the heart of the
Host (D. 3) and the calm of "I kiss my hand to the stars"
(D. 5); and (2) there is—no use denying it—"the terror of
Christ" (D. 2). Christ did not come just to bring peace but
also a sword; He wants his followers to lose their lives, to
take up their crosses, to deny themselves; and when we
share Paul's vision, baptism is not just a matter of getting
rid of original sin or of becoming God's own adopted
child—it implies that we are baptized into conformity

with Christ, suffering, dead, and buried (and hence ris-
en; Romans 6). I cannot think of Hopkins—who went
through the pains of accepting Jesuit formation and
adapting to Jesuit life, and a little later with his obsession
with inscape and instress, and probably the influence of
Newman's distinction between the real and the notional
—that the words of Scripture were to him just words of
Scripture without deeply penetrating (John 8:37). Superficiality was alien to his character; it is the death of
inscape and instress; hence, as I have pointed out a few
times now, his insistence on seriousness and honesty.

In the *Spiritual Exercises*, Ignatius makes the most
arrogant claim, humanly speaking, that "in *these* exercises God communicates directly with the devout person,
enlightening him, embracing him, . . . " (italics mine). To
any good Christian this is downright frightening, and in
my wide experience of conducting the Spiritual Exercises
the retreatant who is open to the Lord—another piece of
advice in the Exercises—at times reaches the point where
he truly feels "scared stiff," and where he knows God is
"The Hound of Heaven," where he instinctively, although subconsciously, reacts: He is winter, but warm;
lightning but love. But the lightning and the winter at
times force him to pray to be delivered from Christ's
terror (D. 3). Whenever I have the responsibility of
clarifying the situation, of helping the devout person
who fears to be *embraced*—which always is and remains
frightening because *God* does the embracing—it is of
little use to show compassion in the form of "I am sorry
for you," and it is totally misplaced and wrong; but one
does come to love this poor person, feeling the frown of
his face as well as the hurtle of hell (D. 3): no way out. So it
has been in my own case when I read *The Wreck of the*

Deutschland. At times my reaction has been: poor fellow, he took his Christianity and his vocation too seriously. Later Hopkins was to write, "this seeing the sick endears them to us" (53); I substitute "suffering, for whatever cause" and feel enriched by my love for Gerard Manley Hopkins.

Every admirer or friend of Hopkins will approach the terrible sonnets with hesitancy, certain misgivings, but also with reverence and awe. Time's eunuch, a lonely began, a man close to despair, knowing himself to be gall, heartburn, his own sweating self worse than those in hell (resp. 74, 66, 64, 67) are not words taken lightly, words that belong in the realm of *beaux lettres.* To move through a life that is comfortless, sheer darkness, amidst cliffs of fall, frightful, sheer, no-man-fathomed is almost beyond comprehension (resp. 69, 67, 65). Poetry here is most certainly not

> What has oft been said,
> But ne'er so well expressed.

The poetry is no more than a means by which man is drawn into close intimacy with a fellow human being wracked by pain. It is now not a matter of sublime sonnets, but of one of ourselves being lonely, despairing, in the dark, comfortless, up against heaven's baffling ban, thwarted in everything by hell's spell (66), and so utterly disappointed that he begs God to give an explanation (74); in brief, a man pitched past pitch of grief (65). Consequently, no one should be so irreverent as to analyse him, to put him on the couch. I can only listen to what he must say, and try to understand, and bless when I do understand (D. 5).

England was to Hopkins "wife to my creating

thought" (66), yet, paradoxically, it was in a foreign country, in Ireland, that he wrote his finest, most profound
verse. He felt a stranger, out of place; he did not like the
work he was asked to do. By now he had been a Jesuit for
some seventeen years and both in his letters and in his
poems we are somewhat painfully startled by the fre-
quency of words like *weary, disappointed, frustrated, jaded,
comfortless,* with nouns like *despair, gall, heartburn, darkness,* with expressions like *ruins of wrecked past purpose, a
tormented mind, a poor potsherd, a winter world.* The one-
thing that he does not refer to is that he is a sinner, and
that consequently he deserves all this. There is an unmistakable distinction between sinners and himself, between
"the sots and thralls of lust" and himself who "spends life,
sir, upon thy cause" (74). It left him with the question
why:

> But ah, but O thou terrible, why wouldst thou rude on me
> Thy wring-world right foot rock? lay a lionlimb against me?
>   scan
> With darksome devouring eyes my bruisèd bones? . . .
>   . . . me frantic to avoid thee and flee? (64)

and again:

> Why do sinners' ways prosper? and why must
> Disappointment all I endeavour end?
> Wert thou my enemy, O thou my friend,
> How wouldst thou worse, I wonder, than thou dost
> Defeat, thwart me? (74)

But no answer is given:

>   . . . And my lament
> Is cries countless, cries like dead letters sent
> To dearest him that lives alas! away (67).

He is up against "dark heaven's baffling ban or hell's spell" (66), where we pay careful attention to the word *baffling*. It is baffling to the poet: it is unlikely that it will be crystal clear to us. In poem 67 he thought that he had found something like an answer:

> I am gall, I am heartburn. God's most just decree
> Bitter would have me taste: my taste was me;

but the fact is that in the final draft of this poem *deep* was substituted for *just*:

> God's most deep decree
> Bitter would have me taste.

This being left in the dark, this receiving no answer, these "countless cries, cries like dead letters" is the bottom line:

> This to hoard unheard,
> Heard unheeded, leaves me a lonely began (66).

The nearest that he thought he came to an answer was when he wrote in *Carrion Comfort*:

> Why? That my chaff might fly; my grain lie, sheer and
>   clear.
> Nay in all that toil, that coil, since (seems) I kissed the rod,
> Hand rather, my heart lo! lapped strength, stole joy, would
>   laugh, chéer.
> Cheer whom though? The hero whose heaven-handling
>   flung me, fóot tród
> Me? or me that fought him? O which one? is it each one?
>   (64)

There is really no letting off: the toil, and coil, and rod, the heaven-handling, the crushing foot are still there, and it is only hindsight that shed light upon his sufferings!

> That night, that year
> Of now done darkness I wretch lay wrestling with (my
>   God!) my God (64).

But to me all that I have brought forward was not made crystal clear by a reference to "now done darkness." Naturally, it reminds us of the opening lines of poem 67:

> I WAKE and feel the fell of dark, not day.
> What hours, O what black hoürs we have spent
> This night! what sights you, heart, saw; ways you went!
> . . . .
> With witness I speak this. But where I say
> Hours I mean years, mean life.

It is a very startling, even shocking question to ask whether Gerard Manley Hopkins, a man of such integrity, honesty, and seriousness, really meant what he wrote. The question sounds like an insult, enough to make one angry. Yet I ask the question: Was Dublin life really a matter of black hours, black years? Was life really a matter of "cliffs of fall frightful, sheer, no-man-fathomed" (65)? He did not want to give in to despair (64), but then why:

> Soul, self; come, poor Jackself, I do advise
> You, jaded, let be; call off thoughts awhile
> Elsewhere . . . (69)

and why:

> The lost are like this, and their scourge to be
> As I am mine, their sweating selves; but worse (67),

74

and surely, when one can only see oneself as "this Jack, joke, poor potsherd, patch, matchwood," one is very, very close to hopelessness and despair.

When I ask these questions, implying a strong suggestion that after all "it was not really that bad," I am not for a moment subtracting even the tiniest morsel from Hopkins's sufferings, in whatever form, of darkness, weariness, frustration, and so on. But I am convinced that there is more to all this, and we find this in the poems themselves, although I do not think that Hopkins himself was aware of what, objectively, is a contradiction: happiness, even peace, in the midst of pain.

He who reads accurately will be faced now and again with apparent contradictions. To take an example: sonnet 67 depicts the poet as lost in darkness; he experiences, notice this verb, God's total absence, he knows himself to be "a lonely began" (66). Yet, in this cruel experience, he refers "to dearest him that lives alas! away" (67). What on earth is happening here? For the darkness is not so dark that he cannot be aware of God living, true, living away; the darkness is evidently not so dark that he cannot still refer to God as "dearest." In sonnet 65 we read the painful lines about the mind with its mountains, its cliffs of fall, sheer, no-man-fathomed, and it certainly looks as if there is no way out:

> Here! creep,
> Wretch, under a comfort serves in a whirlwind: all
> Life death does end and each day dies with sleep.

Yet, was Hopkins aware of a certain contradiction when he in the same sonnet calls upon God:

> Comforter, where, where is your comforting?

75

Or again, in sonnet 69:

> I cast for comfort I can no more get
> By groping round my comfortless, than blind
> Eyes in their dark can day or thirst can find
> Thirst's all-in-all in all a world of wet.

But how can he continue a few lines further on

> ... let joy size

> At God knows when to God knows what; whose smile
> 's not wrung, see you; unforeseen times rather—as skies
> Betweenpie mountains—lights a lovely mile?

These few examples might surely be used to prove that "after all it was not that bad." Can anyone in honesty experience himself as lost, in hell, and yet call God as darkness "dearest"?

Indeed, it just does not make sense; it is not logical. One cannot harmonize the contradictions, and so there appears to be no conclusion but that Hopkins does somewhat exaggerate, that the darkness was not as black as he wants us to believe. However, the answer to these questions and suspicions is that the sufferings were much worse than readers are inclined to think. At this point I am always reminded of a line in *The Wreck of the Deutschland*:

> And here the faithful waver, the faithless fable and miss
> (D. 6),

where Hopkins is making an effort to understand the source of all sufferings in the world.

There was a time when I was wrestling with the problem at hand and thought that I could fall back upon

The Cloud of Unknowing, the well-known medieval treatise on what can happen in prayer, in the intimacy between God and man. But somehow it seemed to me an easy way out. Not that a good deal might not be explained by this treatise, but it was too much of an intellectual approach for a man who was almost dying with pain. I fell back upon the night of the senses and the night of the spirit as explained by St. John of the Cross (1542-91), but it did not satisfy me. It was just too rational to my taste. I experienced some irreverence in trying to understand, and even more, in trying to share the emptiness, the darkness, the bitterness of Gerard Manley Hopkins—and I use on purpose his Christian names. I was reminded of St. Teresa of Avila (1515-82), foundress of many Carmelite convents, who lived some eighteen years in darkness, in total absence of God. Her life made me grasp what God could and did do at times, and I had no difficulty in accepting that this woman, who thought she had lost all faith, could address and inspire her sisters to love God wholeheartedly, without being dishonest, without feeling herself a hypocrite. These and similar approaches struck me as more or less theoretical, true; but theory left me unsatisfied. In humility I fell back upon my own experience.

It is quite often embarrassing to be taken into confidence by a man or a woman, coming to me, opening his or her heart, and building up hopes that I might be able to help, to bring light in darkness, to be comfort in pain, and so forth. At times I could help, at other times I was nowhere, and at a loss myself. Oh, I could give them what I had read in the books, but that usually did not work. Those troubled and suffering people did not want a word from a book, but a word from God, who had disap-

peared from their lives. I soon discerned that I was dealing with a saintly father or mother, a saintly nun or priest.
I listened to what were really tales of woe, dreadful woe.
They had been brought up as good Christians, had lived
Christian lives, had at one time loved God sincerely, were
happy in knowing themselves enriched by God's precious
gift of faith; then, more often than not, inexplicably,
everything had disappeared, everything had been taken
away, without any assignable cause. Frightened to no
end, they told me that they had lost their faith, they no
longer believed in God. After some questions I told them
that the situation was, to say the least, most unpleasant,
that the future would probably be hell, which they admitted. I then asked, or better suggested, "But you won't
blame God, will you?"; to which, before I had finished the
sentence, they answered: "Of course not, it is my own
fault." Going on, I suggested that once in hell they would
not hate God, and again before the sentence was finished
there was the the answer: "Of course not, I will always
love him." I then pointed out that within the span of a few
minutes they had admitted that they no longer believed
in God yet had praised his justice and, hence, his existence, his love, and so on.

It made them see the true light, and convinced them
that things were not bad at all; they just moved in darkness. I knew then and I know now that the word of truth
and of comfort would evaporate completely once they
were on their way home. Their reaction: "No, it is not so;
he has just been very clever; he really never understood
what I was trying to convey." At this point, to explain this
contradictory behavior, I recall the strident words of
Hopkins:

> God's most deep decree
> Bitter would have me taste: *my taste was me* (67);

and there is no reasoning against taste; there is no talking away taste. What had happened in the conversation was that I had addressed myself to this person's intellect, heart, and mind; but all that did not constitute the person in front of me: he, she *was* taste, which by its nature is rather irrational and impervious to argument. In his or her experience, life had become "taste," which stands for conscious experience, completely blocking out the working of head and heart. Blocking out, but the head and heart were there, and it was not difficult to remove the blockage in a simple conversation. But it proved and proves an illusion that in this way what one tastes—which is oneself—is even slightly influenced. But notice the contradiction: the admission that indeed God did exist and that He was not to blame for the darkness. This admission was alive, if that is the right word, on a completely different level of this person's existence. In fact, he or she was not even aware that this level existed, let alone that there could be a living admission clashing headlong with "my taste was me."

This illustration is not exceptional. I am inclined to think that it is deeply human and that it is sooner or later realized in most people. It defies any logical explanation, and even psychology will not move beyond a description of a phenomenon. Any suspicion that there is an exaggeration or lack of honesty in the suffering person only proves that "the faithless fable and miss" (D. 6).

I would like to make one further remark; the very moment any person, including Hopkins, would know what exactly is happening, that God leaves him alone in a desert, or worse, that he has reached some step on the ladder of mystical prayer, would be the end of darkness and sufferings. The suffering soul would now generously, as it were, let God have his way, to a certain extent give God permission to act as he does, would happily keep the situation in hand, even unto being perhaps proud of his docility, of his surrender. Of course, he would not admit this to himself; in fact, he would not be fully aware of it. That is why it is plainly stupid to try to talk anyone out of the emptiness, darkness, the brink of collapsing faith. It might turn out to be an effort to kill the person whose existence is "God's most deep decree bitter would have me taste: my taste is ME." If my friend Gerard Manley Hopkins were to have come to me for some guidance, I would only have admonished him not to change anything in his life, and this with reference to the advice by Ignatius in his *Spiritual Exercises* (whose authority for Hopkins in this situation would be nil: "my taste was me"; not even Ignatius, nor the word of God in Scripture, would be able to turn that around), and I would have prayed like mad that on a next visit "the right word might be given to me" (Ephesians 6). It is not just embarrassing but shattering to give some help to a mind that "has mountains; cliffs of fall frightful, sheer, no-man-fathomed" (65). But I would not make the mistake pointed out by Hopkins: "hold them cheap may who ne'er hung there." Any man who in darkness lies wrestling with (his God!) his God (66) is not even pitied; compassion is not the true reaction. If it were, it would imply that one is judgmental as regards God's dealing (a favorite word with Hopkins) with man. "Pitched past pitch of grief," and do not touch it any more.

No one will be fully satisfied with what I have written in this chapter. If ever he were, he would probably have unknowingly reduced a profound divine mystery to an understandable spiritual phenomenon, and thus have done away with the mystery. That is why humility, reverence, and awe befit any reader when allowed or privileged to share, even to a slight extent, the terror of both the opening stanzas of *The Wreck of the Deutschland* and of the terrible sonnets.

five

"but thou art above, thou Orion of light. . ."

At times the Society founded by Ignatius is depicted as a military *corps d'élite*: easy to explain when supposedly the founder was an ex-soldier. This opinion would explain the kind of formation given to the young recruits: soldiery drill, perhaps even approaching the horrendous *Befehl ist Befehl* of Hitler's days; an order is an order, and one does not think, one does. The person is completely absorbed in the army, in the community. There is only blind obedience, no more. Thus, it is understandable why a man like Hopkins, completely obsessed with the preciousness of inscape, instress, "the self," was forced into sufferings. If only he had wavered in his vocation, which according to his own confession he never did, although humbly he added that he had not lived up to it. This *corps d'élite* could not but narrow down the very concept, and reality, of the life of the Jesuit: serving the Society in its service of the Church. It is as simple as that. A Jesuit without blinkers is unthinkable. Hence, the conflict between Hopkins the very human poet and the Jesuit.

This is a parody, although I am quite willing to admit that Jesuits in the course of the centuries have blundered badly; regrettably, it cannot be set aside as a matter of human weakness.

I would like my readers and admirers of Hopkins to know that the Spiritual Exercises of Ignatius were, and are, never meant to form a soldier but a man of prayer in love with his Lord, a man deeply concerned about the well-being not just of the Catholic Church but of all mankind, in fact of all creation. Throughout the Exercises, from the very beginning until the final contemplation, the devout person is placed in the midst of the whole creation: "all the other things on the face of the earth are created for man to help him in attaining the end for which he is created." This at the beginning. At the end he is to reflect on how God dwells in his creatures: "in the elements giving them existence, in the plants giving them life, in the animals conferring upon them sensation, in men bestowing understanding"; and how He works and labors in all creatures: the heavens, the elements, the plants, the fruits, the cattle, and so on. In another exercise he is to make himself aware of Christ before whom the whole world is assembled. He is asked to see the great extent of the surface of the earth, the whole expanse or circuit of all the earth, inhabited by so many different people, beings so varied, in dress, behavior, color, race, age, well-being, but also so much the same, in great blindness, on their way to death, tempted by Satan. This all-embracing vision was not placed before Hopkins, let us say, only once a year when he spent some eight days in prayer, but was and is part of everyone formed in the school of Ignatius.

This part of the Exercises gives a key to Hopkins's talking about the lovely-asunder starlight, how he could kiss his hand to the stars (D. 5), how spontaneously he would address the earth as "sweet Earth, sweet land-scape" (58), how he would call upon the skies but also upon "rose-moles all in stipple upon trout that swim," and finches' wings, and all things counter, whatever is fickle, and so forth (37). But I have to add at once that this vision always included Him who fathered-forth all this and whose beauty is past change (37), a Christ that plays in ten thousand places (57), that he made an effort "down all that glory in the heavens to glean the Saviour" (38). Now, surely the word *world* has to be taken very seriously when he wrote:

THE world is charged with the grandeur of God (31).

People find difficulty in understanding the not-always-easy language of Hopkins, and they cannot grasp the vision and conviction behind the heavily loaded words and expressions, and especially compounds of the poem about nature as a Heraclitean Fire, "million-fuelèd, na-ture's bonfire burns on" (72). Indeed, Hopkins's aware-ness of whatever is was as wide and unlimited as the sea and the sky, and it was a deeply penetrating vision as is made clear in the wonderfully melodious "Ode to the Night," which he gave the title *Spelt from Sibyl's Leaves* (61).

I have mentioned before that Hopkins is not a romantic poet; I would again add that he was far too honest for it. Indeed, the world was all fathered-forth by Him whose beauty is past change, it is all charged with God's Grandeur; but inscape and instress made it impossible for him to be blind to the glaring fact that "all is seared with trade, bleared, smeared with toil, and wears man's smudge and shares man's smell" (31), that this "rich round world" looks bare, and "wears brows of such care and dear concern" (58). I spoke about this in my chapter on his dear aspens. I have tried to place it now in a wider perspective; and there is a shift from the damage done, to man who does the damage. There is now the strident confession that nature's "bonniest, dearest to her, her clearest-selvèd spark, man" is "in an unfathomable, all is in an enormous dark drowned" (72). Strident, because of "what are love's worthiest . . . world's loveliest—men's selves" (62). He is now filled with pity for "the comfortless unconfessed" (D. 31); there is the thoughtful complaint

> . . . our curse
> Of ruinous shrine no hand or, worse,
>   Robbery's hand is busy to
> Dress, hoar-hallowèd shrines unvisited;
> . . . .
>   These daredeaths, ay this crew, in
> Unchrist, all rolled in ruin—
>
> Deeply surely I need to deplore it,
> Wondering why my master bore it,
>   The riving off that race
> So at home, time was, to his truth and grace
> That a starlight-wender of ours would say
> The marvellous Milk was Walsingham Way . . . (L. 89-102).

The poet can still write of "dear man," but pitifully he adds "dogged" and then continues:

Ah, the heir
To his own selfbent so bound, so tied to his turn,
To thriftless reave both our rich round world bare
And none reck of world after . . . (58).

One must try to gather together the various aspects of creation or nature—on the one hand charged with the Grandeur of God and entrusted to world's loveliest, men's selves, and on the other so much smeared and smudged, and man, nature's bonniest, dearest spark, drowned in an enormous dark, and God no longer gleaned from amidst nature's beauty, just because the beholder is wanting, because man, the inmate, does not correspond—in order to even slightly understand how his sufferings are not self-ish (notice the hyphen) but how his "cries heave, herds-long, huddle in a main, a chief-woe, world-sorrow" (65). I by no means find it easy to grasp fully Hopkins's sorrow and I am reminded once again

And here the faithful waver, the faithless fable and miss
(D. 6).

The depth of Hopkins's vision is, in my conviction, not shared by many, if by any; it is, alas, not shared by me. His self is too rich, too great, too majestic, perhaps, paradoxically, too simple, which might just be what makes him as lovable as he is. The poet had many, many reasons for being a gloomy person; and with all the weariness, frustration, near-despair, darkness, empti-ness, loneliness, a genuine pessimist. The miracle is that the opposite is true. Where there is lightning, he still discerns love; where it is cold, he still feels the warmth (D. 9). Where God's Grandeur is maimed and marred so that everything wears man's smudge, he is unshaken in his belief and his vision that "for all this, there lives the dearest freshness deep down things" (31; where I would once again urge the reader of Hopkins's poetry to notice how fond he is of the adjective *dear*, how often it occurs, and how often in unexpected places). The black West, and it makes him, with a joyful *Oh*, think of morning, springing at the brown brink eastward (31)! Where the inmate is blind to "all the air things wear that build this world of Wales," there is no judgment or condemnation, but a prayer that God, a lover of souls, swaying considerate scales—notice the gentle, mellow impact of *considerate*—may complete his creature dear (notice *dear*, notwithstanding that he does not correspond), "being mighty a master, being a father and fond" (34). I almost added: the optimist! He is aware that

> . . . We, life's pride and cared-for crown,
> Have lost that cheer and charm of earth's past prime:
> Our make and making break, are breaking, down
> To man's last dust, drain fast towards man's first slime
> (35).

And yet, no matter whom,

> Christ minds: Christ's interest, what to avow or amend
> There, éyes them, heart wánts, care haúnts, foot
> fóllows kînd,
> Their ránsom, théir rescue, ánd first, fást, last friénd
> (40).

It is surely surprising that pained by the shipwreck, by the death of the sisters, and another fifty victims, "two hundred souls in the round . . . of a fourth the doom to be

drowned" (D. 12), he did trace the presence of a lovely-
felicitous Providence, which made him ask the question

> is the shipwrack then a harvest,
> does tempest carry the grain for thee? (D. 31)

Within a year of his death, in October 1888, Hopkins's vision appears to be deeply comprehensive. He
embraces the whole of nature, places special emphasis on
man, in a special way the tragedy of man (remember:
"nature's bonniest, dearest to her, her clearest-selvèd
spark, man"), which makes him sigh, "O pity and indig-
nation" and the reason:

> . . . Manshape, that shone
> Sheer off, disseveral, a star, | death blots black out:
> nor mark
> Is any of him at all so stark
> But vastness blurs and time | beats level (72).

What is left over is "this Jack, joke, poor potsherd, patch,
matchwood." Hopkins then wants to stop this and cries
out "enough" and we witness the shocking reversal of
another experience when "all life death does end and
each day dies with sleep" (65). Now it is all death life does
end, and each day lives forever: "Enough! the Resurrec-
tion. . . . Across my foundering deck shone a beacon, an
eternal beam . . . " and matchwood is now immortal
diamond (72).

Hopkins once wrote to Patmore about Scotus, and
his comment was: he saw too far, he knew too much. I
think this is applicable to the poet himself. And when he
calls Scotus "of realty the rarest-veinèd unraveller; a not
rivalled insight" (44), it is to me as if I am reading about
Hopkins himself. This might seem to be an insoluble

paradox, for both Hopkins and Scotus were passionately concerned about the self, indeed, one's own self, man's self, but only insofar as man's self is the most precious of selves in the whole of creation. I refer the reader once again to the poem about Nature as a Heraclitean Fire (72). But the self of his aspens dear as well as the self of his lovely-asunder starlight and of everything in between has something majestic. After all, it is fathered-forth by Him whose beauty is beyond change. In this vastness of creation man is on the one hand a speck, a piece of matchwood, but on the other hand he is immortal diamond, for whom all the other things of creation were made. But the past tense is wrong; the sentence should read "for whom all other things are being made"; after all, they *are*, not *were*, fathered-forth by Him whose beauty is beyond change. Hence, back again to his vision that Nature is a burning fire.

Now, it is not difficult for me to give my assent to this truth, but in my case it would be to a very high degree notional, making use of Newman's distinction; it would be real and alive for me only to a very limited extent. It is here that Hopkins, in spite of all his sufferings, belongs to the great visionaries of all time, although such an assessment would surprise, even shock, him to no end. To him it came naturally; there was no problem; it was just plain unshakable truth:

... thou art above, thou Orion of light (D. 21).

For quite a long time I considered it a legend, a pious one, that on his deathbed Hopkins was heard to say, "I am so happy, I am so happy." I could not find the source in Mrs. Phare's slender volume on Hopkins (1933). Anyway, the impression was given that close to death Hopkins was privileged to shed all darkness and to move into the light, a foretaste of eternal light awaiting him. The impression was given that the lightning had disappeared and only love remained, that there was no more winter but only warmth (D. 9). The impression was given that peacefully, even joyfully he gave his life back to the Lord, which is certainly something when you are only forty-four years old. The words drag with them a shadow of suggestion that he was glad it was all over. I found it very difficult to accept this interpretation of those last words.

However, the words are no legend—they are authentic. Because the last hours of any friend are very precious, I cannot but have my readers share what was written by one of Gerard's most intimate friends, who saw a great deal of him during the last two or three years of his life. It is part of the obituary notice published in what we might call a newsletter destined for Jesuits only:

A day or two after Low Sunday, 1889, he fell ill of typhoid fever. From the outset, he was fully alive to the gravity of his state, and, I believe, never shared the hope that others from time to time entertained, that he would pull through.

During the night of Wednesday, the 5th of June, a serious change for the worse took place in his condition, and when the doctors arrived early next morning, they pronounced his case well-nigh desperate. Father Wheeler, S.J., who attended him all through his illness with affectionate care, told him of his danger, and gave him the Holy Viaticum, which he received with the deepest devotion.

On hearing that his parents were coming from England, he appeared to dread their arrival, because of the pain it would give them to see him so prostrate, but when the first interview was over, he expressed the happiness he felt at having them with him.

He quite realized that he was dying, and asked each day for the Holy Viaticum. He received It for the last time on the morning of the day of his death, Saturday, the 8th of June.

The final blessing and absolution were also then given him at his own request, and he was heard two or three times to say, 'I am so happy, I am so happy.' Soon afterwards, he became too weak to speak, but he appeared to follow mentally the prayers for the dying, which were said a little before noon by Father Wheeler, and joined in by his parents. As the end approached he seemed to grow more collected, and retained consciousness almost up to the moment, half-past one o'clock, when he passed peacefully away.

Hopkins truly spoke these precious words, and we have to accept a pretty sudden change in his fortune; two months earlier he was still pleading with his God: "why do sinners' ways prosper? and why must disappointment all I endeavour end?" (74). A month or a little more before his death he dedicates the last sonnet we have to Robert Bridges and complains about his "winter world," about his soul's needing so much "the sweet fire the sire of muse," wanting so much "the one rapture of an inspiration" (76). Is it possible that an abundance of comfort was poured over him by One whom he once called "Hero of Calvary" (D. 8)? I doubt it. Surveying the poet's life and his poetry, I am reminded of the privilege not merely to believe in Christ but to suffer for his sake (Philippians 1:29). Above we heard his own words that to ask to be lifted to a higher state of grace was to ask to be lifted to a higher cross, and he believed that baptism implied conformity with the Son of God, suffering, dead, buried (Romans 6: 1-6). Is there a reminder of the nun's calling "O Christ, come quickly," with its unforgettable conclusion:

> The cross to her she calls Christ to her, christens her
> wild-worst
> Best?

Best, and a proper name, and hence

> Beyond saying sweet, past telling of tongue (D. 9).

As I read Hopkins, "I am so happy" is not the undoing, nor the end of his sufferings; it is his wounded self claiming victory over all his pain. But again, feeling close to a friend, dying some seven weeks before his forty-fifth birthday, after a six-week illness, and after a life clearly marked by pain in various forms, I cannot conceive of his last words as expressing reward. They express victory; they are a "heart's-clarion" (72). It fills me with awe at his greatness and majesty; but then majesty is goodness soaked in simplicity, and I am back in the second chapter: the child that Gerard Manley Hopkins was and remained throughout his life and that went hidden behind the irresistible urge and doomed-to-failure effort "to word it," which could only be worded "by Him that present and past, heaven and earth are word of, worded by" (D. 29).

Summarizing, I heard much about darkness, in the shape of a black-about air (D. 24), of pain without comfort (69), of a foundering deck (72), of a winter world (76), of hope that had grown grey hairs, wearing mourning (D. 15), and in many other very diverse shapes. However, with his poems in my head and in my heart, I always know that to Hopkins there was the unblurred vision:

> but thou art above, thou Orion of Light.

epilogue

To close this unpretentious tribute with an epilogue
might strike the reader as somewhat pompous. The reason that I take this risk is that I cherish the hope my
tribute might in some way be a contribution, not necessarily to Hopkins scholarship, but to a more profound
knowledge of Hopkins's poetry and, especially, to a
greater love for the poet. But I am aware that possibly I
have put up barriers that prevent such a fortunate by-
product from coming about.

I fear that I may have used too many quotations and
thus given the impression that periodically I was trying to
prove a point, or, worse, making apologies for oddities

and obscurities, or putting up a defense against ir-
regularities, indefensible rhymes, unnecessary distor-
tions of grammar and syntax, this in an indirect way by
never touching upon them, as if there were not any.
Some readers may have very serious objections to the way
in which I have handled lines from Hopkins's poetry:
jumping around, without any deference as to *where* or
when a particular poem from which the quotation is taken
was written. I take such objections seriously myself. Is it
legitimate to illustrate what happened in the Dublin years
by indiscriminately referring to what the poet experienced and wrote when he was studying theology? Or the
other way around: is it honest, fair practice to elucidate
what happened to Hopkins as a young priest by boldly
falling back upon his experience of some ten years later?
And so I had to add an epilogue to safeguard the
genuineness of my tribute.

I do not think that I am guilty of "jumping around"
for whatever reason. But I cannot see the life of Hopkins
as just a succession of days and weeks, that is, as a series of
events, of experiences, of successes or disappointments,
in which each new experience pushes the previous one
out of the way, more or less to oblivion. To a large extent
this is common practice in our culture; the hectic pace of
living often leaves no choice. Then there is the worldly
but frequently inhuman wisdom of "She (or he) should
by now be over it," or "Pull yourself together: life has to
go on," and similar pieces of irresponsible advice. We are
familiar with these approaches, disastrous, however well
meant. They are ultimately all an invitation to become
superficial by dropping the past in order to move on. But
the past is always with us, unless we join the hectic pace
and cut ourselves off from what is an essential part of our

very existence. Hopkins's obsession with inscape and in-stress was not a matter at all of self-occupation, of being, perhaps in a sickly manner, occupied with his *self*; it was his defense against superficiality and against the lie that the past is over and done with, dead. Hence, when I give the impression of being blind to days and years, it is because all those days and years are still very much *today*. It may be a matter of "now done darkness"; however, the pain of wrestling with his God left not just a scar but a wound that in moments of withdrawal, of being more intensely his own *self*, would still hurt. This explains why in his terrible sonnets of 1884-89 we find many echoes of what he wrote some ten years before.

In this connection I believe that the fact that, with a few exceptions, none of his poetry was published when he was still alive was a blessing in disguise. Publication somehow rounds off the creative process; it is tied down to pages held together by covers. The product can now be sold and a place given on a bookshelf. One can move on to the next treatise, novel, poem, and so forth. But if there is the disappointment of what the poet considers valuable, inspiring, beautiful, lying idly in the drawer of the desk, the situation changes: the poem—to restrict myself to this—is now marked "rejected"; and probably because it has been rejected, it will become so much the dearer to the poet.

In a happily fortuitous way this is confirmed in the last poem Hopkins wrote to his friend Bridges as well as in the sonnet the latter wrote when some thirty years after Hopkins's death he published the poems. A month before his death Hopkins describes what happened to him when he experienced "the fine delight that fathers thought; the strong spur that breathes once and quenched faster than it came leaves yet the mind a mother of immortal song" (76):

> Nine months she then, nay years, nine years she long
> Within her wears, bears, cares and combs the same.

Elsewhere I rejected a suggestion of Bridges that sooner or later Hopkins would have changed *combs* to *moulds*; I would just now draw attention to the adjective *long*, with all the overtones of the verb *to long*, as well as to the somewhat strange choice of *wears* followed by the correct choice of *bears*. The verbal form *wears* suggested and is connected with *weary*, and the preceding *long* almost demands *weary*, the more so because there is question of nine years. Now, pursuing Hopkins's imagery, when a mother has longingly borne her child for nine long months, the *caring* and the *combing* do not cease when the child is born. And we know that Hopkins touched and retouched his poems. But this can only mean that neither the inspiration nor the poem was ever past: the mind is forever "a mother of immortal song" (76). The unpublished poems were not idly lying in his desk, but were lovingly preserved by Bridges. His poems were never writings of the past, but were ever alive within him. If this is true, then there is no "jumping around" from present to past and *vice versa*; there is a reverent contemplation of Hopkins's *oeuvre*, never split into pieces by dates.

I here share the vision of Bridges when he published Hopkins's poems. In the sonnet preceding them he wrote:

> OUR generation already is overpast,
> And thy lov'd legacy, Gerard, hath lain
> Coy in my home. . . .
> . . . .

Hell wars without; but, dear, the while my hands
Gather'd thy book, I heard, this wintry day,
Thy spirit thank me. . . .
. . . .
Go forth: amidst our chaffinch flock display
Thy plumage of far wonder and heavenward flight!

Poem in the singular or in the plural does not occur. It has
been a matter of gathering pages into a book, which is
cherished as a legacy, and let go into the wide world like a
bird, displaying its feathers, its free flight. But the most
important sentence to me is "I heard thy spirit thank me,"
which can only mean that his friend-poet, more than his
poems, is given to another generation. I could not agree
more. Hence, this tribute to a simple, loveable man, coming to us through his *oeuvre*, which through God's feathery Providence lay hidden for a whole generation.